GRAY

BY

EDMUND GOSSE

AMS PRESS
NEW YORK

Reprinted from the edition of 1889, London
First AMS EDITION published 1968
Manufactured in the United States of America

Library of Congress Catalogue Card Number: 68-58380

74871

AMS PRESS, INC.
New York, N.Y. 10003

PREFATORY NOTE.

As a biographical study, this little volume differs in one important respect from its predecessors in this series. Expansion, instead of compression, has had to be my method in treating the existing lives of Gray. Of these, none have hitherto been published except in connexion with some part of his works, and none has attempted to go at all into detail. Mitford's, which is the fullest, would occupy, in its purely biographical section, not more than thirty of these pages.

The materials I have used are chiefly taken from the following sources : —

I. The *Life and Letters of Gray*, edited by Mason in 1775. This work consists of a very meagre thread of biography connecting a collection of letters, which would be more valuable, if Mason had not tampered with them, altering, omitting, and re-dating at his own free will.

II. Mitford's *Life of Thomas Gray*, prefixed to the 1814 edition of the *Poems*. This is very valuable so far as it goes. The Rev. John Mitford was a young clergyman who was born ten years after the death of Gray, and who made it the business of his life to collect from such survivors as remembered Gray all the documents and anecdotes that he could secure. This is the life which was altered and enlarged, to be prefixed to the Eton Gray, in 1845.

III. Mitford's Edition of the *Works* of Gray, published
in 4 vols., in 1836. This contained the genuine text of
most of the letters printed by Mason, and a large number
which now saw the light for the first time, addressed to
Wharton, Chute, Nicholls, and others.

IV. Correspondence and Reminiscences of the Rev.
Norton Nicholls, edited by Mitford, in 1843.

V. The *Correspondence of Gray and Mason*, to which
are added other letters, not before printed, an exceedingly
valuable collection, not widely enough known, which was
published by Mitford in 1853.

VI. The *Works* of Gray, as edited in 2 vols., by Mathias,
in 1814 ; this is the only publication in which the Pembroke MSS. have hitherto been made use of.

VII. *Souvenirs de C. V. de Bonstetten*, 1832.

VIII. The Correspondence of Horace Walpole.

IX. Gray's and Stonehewer's MSS., as preserved in
Pembroke College, Cambridge.

X. MS. Notes and Letters by Gray, Cole, and others,
in the British Museum.

By far the best account of Gray, not written by a personal friend, is the brief summary of his character and
genius contributed by Mr. Matthew Arnold to " The
English Poets."

No really good or tolerably full edition of Gray's *Works*
is in existence. Neither his English nor his Latin Poems
have been edited in any collection which is even approxi-
mately complete ; and his Letters, although they are
better given by Mitford than by Mason, are very far from
being in a satisfactory condition. In many of them the
date is wrongly printed ; and some which bear no date,
are found, by internal evidence to be incorrectly attributed
by Mitford. No attempt has ever been made to collect

Gray's writings into one single publication. I am sorry to say that all my efforts to obtain a sight of Gray's unpublished letters and facetious poems, many of which were sold at Sotheby and Wilkinson's, on the 4th of August, 1854, have failed. On the other hand, the examination of the Pembroke MSS. has supplied me with a considerable amount of very exact and important biographical information which has never seen the light until now.

I have to express my warmest thanks to the Master and Fellows of Pembroke College, Cambridge, who permitted me to examine these invaluable MSS.; to Mr. R. A. Neil, of Pembroke, and Mr. J. W. Clark, of Trinity, whose kindness in examining archives, and copying documents for me, has been great; to the late Mr. R. S. Turner, who has placed his Gray MSS. at my disposal; to Professor Sidney Colvin and Mr. Basil Champneys, who have given me the benefit of their advice on those points of art and architecture which are essential to a study of Gray; and to Mr. Edward Scott, and Mr. Richard Garnett, for valuable assistance in the Library of the British Museum. For much help in forming an idea of the world in which Gray moved, I am indebted to Mr. Christopher Wordsworth's books on Cambridge in the eighteenth century.

March 1882.

To the above statement I may briefly add that in 1884 I had the pleasure of editing for Messrs. Macmillan and Co., the entire *Works* of Gray, in 4 volumes. In an appendix to this volume I have given a few biographical facts which have come to my knowledge since 1882.

Christmas 1886.

CONTENTS.

CHAPTER VIII.

CHAPTER IX.

CHAPTER X.

GRAY

GRAY.

CHAPTER I.

CHILDHOOD AND EARLY COLLEGE LIFE.

THOMAS GRAY was born at his father's house in Cornhill, on the 26th of December, 1716. Of his ancestry nothing is known. Late in life, when he was a famous poet, Baron Gray of Gray in Forfarshire claimed him as a relation, but with characteristic serenity he put the suggestion from him. " I know no pretence," he said to Beattie, "that I have to the honour Lord Gray is pleased to do me ; but if his Lordship chooses to own me, it certainly is not my business to deny it." The only proof of his connexion with this ancient family is that he possessed a bloodstone seal, which had belonged to his father, engraved with Lord Gray's arms, gules a Lion rampant, within a bordure engrailed argent. These have been accepted at Pembroke College as the poet's arms, but as a matter of fact we may say that he sprang on both sides from the lower-middle classes. His paternal grandfather had been a successful merchant, and died leaving Philip, apparently his only son, a fortune of 10,000*l.* Through various vicissitudes this money passed, at length almost

B

reaching the poet's hands in no very much diminished
quantity, for Philip Gray seems to have been as clever
in business as he was extravagant.   He was born
July 27, 1676.   Towards his thirtieth year he married
Miss Dorothy Antrobus, a Buckinghamshire lady, about
twenty years of age, who, with her sister Mary, a young
woman three years her senior, kept a milliner's shop in
the city.   They belonged, however, to a genteel family,
for the remaining sister, Anna, was the wife of a prosperous country lawyer, Mr. Jonathan Rogers, and the two
brothers, Robert and Thomas Antrobus, were fellows of
Cambridge colleges, and afterwards tutors at Eton.
These five persons take a prominent place in the subse-
quent life of the poet, whereas he never mentions any of
the Grays.   His father had certainly one sister, Mrs.
Oliffe, a woman of violent temper, who married a gentleman of Norfolk, and was well out of the way till after
the death of Gray's mother, when she began to haunt
him, and only died two or three months before he did.
She seems to have resembled Philip Gray in character,
for the poet, always singularly respectful and loyal to his
other elderly relations, calls her "the Spawn of Cerberus
upon the Dragon of Wantley."

Dorothy Gray was unfortunate in her married life ;
her husband was violent, jealous, and probably mad.
Of her twelve children, Thomas was the only one
whom she reared, but Mason is doubtless wrong in
saying that the eleven who died were all suffocated
by infantile convulsions.   Mrs. Gray speaks in her
"case" of the expense of providing "all manner of
apparel for her children."   Thomas, however, certainly
would have died as an infant, but that his mother, finding
him in a fit, opened a vein with her scissors, by that

means relieving the determination of blood to the brain. His father neglected him, and he was brought up by his mother and his aunt Mary. He also mentions with touching affection, in speaking of the death of a Mrs. Bonfoy in 1763, that "she taught me to pray." Home life at Cornhill was rendered miserable by the cruelties of the father, and it seems that the boy's uncle, Robert Antrobus, took him away to his own house at Burnham, in Bucks. This gentleman was a fellow of Peterhouse, as his younger brother Thomas was of King's College, Cambridge. With Robert the boy studied botany, and became learned, according to Horace Walpole, in the virtues of herbs and simples. Unfortunately this uncle died on January 23, 1729, at the age of fifty; there still exists a copy of *Waller's Poems*, in which Gray has written his own name, with this date; perhaps it was an heirloom of his uncle.

In one of Philip Gray's fits of extravagance he seems to have had a full-length of his son painted, about this time, by the fashionable portrait-painter of the day, Jonathan Richardson the elder. This picture is now in the Fitzwilliam Museum at Cambridge. The head is good in colour and modelling; a broad pale brow, sharp nose and chin, large eyes, and a pert expression give a lively idea of the precocious and not very healthy young gentleman of thirteen. He is dressed in a blue satin coat, lined with pale shot silk, and crosses his stockinged legs so as to display dapper slippers of russet leather. His father, however, absolutely refused to educate him, and he was sent to Eton, about 1727, under the auspices of his uncles, and at the expense of his mother. On the 26th of April of the same year, a smart child of ten with the airs of a little dancing-master, a child who

was son of a prime minister, and had kissed the king's
hand, entered the same school ; and some intellectual impulse brought them together directly in a friendship that
was to last, with a short interval, until the death of one of
them more than forty years afterwards.

It is not certain that Horace Walpole at once adopted that
attitude of frivolous worship which he preserved towards
Gray in later life. He was a brilliant little social meteor
at Eton, and Gray was probably attracted first to him.
Yet it was characteristic of the poet throughout life that
he had always to be sought, and even at Eton his talents
may have attracted Walpole's notice. At all events, they
became fast friends, and fostered in one another intellectual pretensions of an alarming nature. Both were oppi-
dans and not collegers, and therefore it is difficult to trace
them minutely at Eton. But we know that they "never
made an expedition against bargemen, or won a match
at cricket," for this Walpole confesses ; but they wandered
through the playing-fields at Eton tending a visionary
flock, and "sighing out some pastoral name to the echo of
the cascade under the bridge" which spans Chalvey
Brook. An avenue of lime among the elms is still
named the "Poet's Walk," and is connected by tradition with Gray. They were a pair of weakly little
boys, and in these days of brisk athletic training
would hardly be allowed to exist. Another amiable and
gentle boy, still more ailing than themselves, was early
drawn to them by sympathy : this was Richard West, a
few months younger than Gray and older than Walpole, a
son of the Richard West who was made Lord Chancellor
of Ireland when he was only thirty-five, and who then
immediately died ; his mother's father, dead before young
Richard's birth, had been the famous Bishop Gilbert Bur-

net.   A fourth friend was Thomas Ashton, who soon slips out of our history, but who survived until 1775.

These four boys formed a " quadruple alliance " of the warmest friendship. West seemed the genius among them; he was a nervous and precocious lad, who made verses in his sleep, cultivated not only a public Latin Muse, but also a private English one, and dazzled his companions by the ease and fluency of his pen. His poetical remains, to which we shall presently return, since they are intimately connected with the development of Gray's genius, are of sufficient merit to permit us to believe that had he lived he might have achieved a reputation among the minor poets of his age. Neither Shenstone nor Beattie had written anything so considerable when they reached the age at which West died. His character was extremely winning, and in his correspondence with Gray, as far as it has been preserved, we find him at first the more serious and the more affectionate friend. But the symptoms of his illness, which seem to have closely resembled those of Keats, destroyed the superficial sweetness of his nature, and towards the end we find Gray the more sober and the more manly of the two.

Besides the inner circle of Walpole, West, and Ashton, there was an outer ring of Eton friends, whose names have been preserved in connexion with Gray's. Among these was George Montagu, grand-nephew of the great Earl of Halifax ; Stonehewer, a very firm and loyal friend, with whom Gray's intimacy deepened to the end of his life ; Clarke, afterwards a fashionable physician at Epsom ; and Jacob Bryant, the antiquary, whose place in class was next to Gray's through one term. With these he doubtless shared those delights of swimming, birds'-nesting, hoops and trap-ball, which he has described,

in ornate eighteenth-century fashion, in the famous stanza
of his Eton Ode :—

> Say, Father Thames, for thou hast seen
>   Full many a sprightly race,
> Disporting on thy margent green,
>   The paths of pleasure trace ;
> Who foremost now delights to cleave,
> With pliant arm, thy glassy wave,
>   The captive linnet which enthral ?
> What idle progeny succeed
> To chase the rolling circle's speed,
>   Or urge the flying ball ?

But we have every reason to believe that he was much
more amply occupied in helping " grateful Science " to
adore " her Henry's holy shade."   Learning was still
preferred to athletics at our public schools, and Gray
was naturally drawn by temperament to study.   It has
always been understood that he versified at Eton, but the
earliest lines of his which have hitherto been known are
as late as 1736, when he had been nearly two years at
Cambridge.   I was, however, fortunate enough to
find among the MSS. in Pembroke College a "play
exercise at Eton," in the poet's handwriting, which had
never been printed, and which is valuable as showing us
the early ripeness of his scholarship.   It is a theme, in
seventy-three hexameter verses, commencing with the
line—

> Pendet Homo incertus gemini ad confinia mundi.

The normal mood of man is described as one of hesi-
tation between the things of Heaven and the things of
Earth ; he assumes that all nature is made for his enjoyment, but soon experience steps in and proves to him the
contrary ; he endeavours to fathom the laws of nature,

but their scheme evades him, and he learns that his effort is a futile one. The proper study of mankind is man, and yet how narrow a theme! Man yearns for ever after superhuman power and accomplishment, only to discover the narrow scope of his possibilities, and he has at last to curb his ambition, and be contented with what God and nature have ordained. The thoughts are beyond a boy, though borrowed in the main from Horace and Pope ; while the verse is still more remarkable, being singularly pure and sonorous, though studded, in boyish fashion, with numerous tags from Virgil. What is really noticeable about this early effusion, is the curious way in which it prefigures its author's maturer moral and elegiac manner ; we see the writer's bias and the mode in which he will approach ethical questions, and we detect in this little " play-exercise " a shadow of the stately didactic reverie of the *Odes*. As this poem has never been described, I may be permitted to quote a few of the verses :—

> Plurimus (hic error, demensque libido lacessit)
> In superos cœlumque ruit, sedesque relinquit,
> Quas natura dedit proprias, jussitque tueri.
> Humani sortem generis pars altera luget,
> Invidet armento, et campi sibi vindicat herbam.
> O quis me in pecoris felicia transferet arva,
> In loca pastorum deserta, atque otia dia ?
> Cur mihi non Lyncisne oculi, vel odora canum vis
> Additur, aut gressus cursu glomerare potestas ?
> Aspice ubi, teneres dum texit aranea casses,
> Funditur in telam, et late per stamina vivit !
> Quid mihi non tactus eadem exquisita facultas
> Taurorumve tori solidi, pennæve volucrum.

In the face of such lines as these, and bearing in mind Walpole's assertion that " Gray never was a boy," we may form a tolerably exact idea of the shy and studious lad, already a scholar and a moralist, moving somewhat gravely and precociously through the classes of that venerable college which has since adopted him as her typical child, and which now presents to each emerging pupil a handsome selection from the works of the Etonian *par excellence*, Thomas Gray.

In 1734, the quadruple alliance broke up. Gray, and probably Ashton, proceeded to Cambridge, where the former was for a short time a pensioner of Pembroke Hall, but went over, on the 3rd of July, still as a pensioner, to his uncle Antrobus' College, Peterhouse.[1] Walpole went up to London for the winter, and did not make his appearance at King's College, Cambridge, until March, 1735. West, meanwhile, had been isolated from his friends by being sent to Oxford, where he entered Christ Church much against his will. For a year the young undergraduates are absolutely lost to sight. If they wrote to one another, their letters are missing, and the correspondence of Walpole and of Gray with West begins in November 1735.

But in the early part of that year a very striking incident occurred in the Gray family, an incident that was perfectly unknown until, in 1807, a friend of Haslewood's happened to discover, in a volume of MS. lawcases, a case submitted by Mrs. Dorothy Gray to the eminent civilian John Audley, in February 1735. In

[1] The Master of Peterhouse has kindly copied for me, from the register of admissions at that college, this entry, hitherto inedited:—" Jul : 3tio· 1734. Thomas Gray Middlesexiensis in scholâ publicâ Etonensi institutus, annosque natus 18 (petente Tutore suo) censetur admisus ad Mensam Pensionariorum sub Tutore et Fidejussore Mro· Birkett, sed ea lege ut brevi se sistat in collegio et examinatoribus se probet."

this extraordinary document the poet's mother states that for nearly thirty years, that is to say for the whole of her married life, she has received no support from her husband, but has depended entirely on the receipts of the shop kept by herself and her sister, moreover "almost providing everything for her son, whilst at Eton school, and now he is at Peter-House in Cambridge."

Notwithstanding which, almost ever since he (her husband) hath been married, he hath used her in the most inhuman manner, by beating, kicking, punching, and with the most vile and abusive language, that she hath been in the utmost fear and danger of her life, and hath been obliged this last year to quit her bed, and lie with her sister. This she was resolved, if possible, to bear; not to leave her shop of trade for the sake of her son, to be able to assist in the maintainance of him at the University, since his father won't.

Mrs. Gray goes on to state that her husband has an insane jealousy of all the world, and even of her brother Thomas Antrobus, and that he constantly threatens "to ruin himself to undo her, and his only son," having now gone so far as to give Mary Antrobus notice to quit the shop in Cornhill at Midsummer next. If he carries out this threat, Mrs. Gray says that she must go with her sister, to help her "in the said trade, for her own and her son's support." She asks legal counsel which way will be best "for her to conduct herself in this unhappy circumstance." Mr. Audley writes sympathetically from Doctor's Commons, but civilly and kindly tells her that she can find no protection in the English law.

This strange and tantalising document, the genuineness of which has never been disputed, is surrounded by difficulties to a biographer. The known wealth and

occasional extravagances of Philip Gray make it hard to
understand why he should be so rapacious of his wife's
little earnings, and at the same time so barbarous in his
neglect of her and of his son. That there is not one
word or hint of family troubles in Gray's copious correspondence is what we might expect from so proud and
reticent a nature. But the gossipy Walpole must have
known all this, and Mason need not have been so excessively discreet, when all concerned had long been
dead. Perhaps Mrs. Gray exaggerated a little, and
perhaps also the vileness of her husband's behaviour in
1735 made her forget that in earlier years they had
lived on gentler terms. At all events, the money-
scrivener is shown to have been miserly, violent, and, as
I have before conjectured, probably half-insane. The
interesting point in the whole story is Mrs. Gray's self-
sacrifice for her son, a devotion which he in his turn
repaid with passionate attachment, and remembered with
tender effusion to the day of his death. He inherited
from his mother his power of endurance, his quiet recti-
tude, his capacity for suffering in silence, and the singular
tenacity of his affections.

Gray, Ashton and Horace Walpole were at Cambridge
together as undergraduates from the spring of 1735 until
the winter of 1738. They associated very much with
one another, and Walpole shone rather less it would
appear than at any other part of his life. The following
extract of a letter from Walpole to West, dated November 9, 1735, is particularly valuable :—

Tydeus rose and set at Eton. He is only known here to be a
scholar of King's. Orosmades and Almanzor are just the same ;
that is, I am almost the only person they are acquainted with,
and consequently the only person acquainted with their excel-

lencies. Plato improves every day; so does my friendship with him. These three divide my whole time, though I believe you will guess there is no quadruple alliance; that is a happiness which I only enjoyed when you was at Eton.

The nick-name which gives us least difficulty here is that in which we are most interested. Orosmades was West's name for Gray, because he was such a chilly mortal, and worshipped the sun. West himself was known as Favonius. Tydeus is very clearly Walpole himself, and Almanzor is probably Ashton. I would hazard the conjecture that Plato is Henry Coventry, a young man then making some stir in the University with certain semi-religious *Dialogues*. He was a friend of Ashton's, and produced on Horace Walpole a very startling impression, causing in that volatile creature for the first and only time an access of fervent piety, during which Horace actually went to read the Bible to the prisoners in the Castle gaol. Very soon this wore off, and Coventry himself became a free-thinker, but Ashton remained serious, and taking orders very early, dropped out of the circle of friends. In all this the name of Gray is not mentioned, but one is justified in believing that he did not join the reading-parties at the Castle.

Early in 1736 the three Cambridge undergraduates appeared in print simultaneously and for the first time in a folio collection of Latin *Hymeneals* on the marriage of Frederic, Prince of Wales. Of these effusions, Gray's copy of hexameters is by far the best, and was so recognized from the first. Mason has thought it necessary to make a curious apology for this poem, and says that Gray " ought to have been above prostituting his powers " in " adulatory verses of this kind." But if he had glanced through the lines again, of which he must have

been speaking from memory, Mason would have seen
that they contain no more fulsome compliments than
were absolutely needful on the occasion. The young
poet is not thinking at all about their royal highnesses,
but a great deal about his own fine language, and is very
innocent of anything like adulation. The verses themselves do not show much progress; there is a fine
passage at the end, but it is almost a cento from Ovid.
One line, melancholy to relate, does not scan. In every
way superior to the *Hymeneal* is *Luna Habitabilis*, a
poem in nearly one hundred verses, written by desire of
the College in 1737, and printed in the *Musæ Etonenses*.
It is impossible to lay any stress on these official productions, mere exercises on a given text. At Pembroke,
both in the library of the College, and in the Stonehewer
MSS. at the master's lodge, I have examined a number of
similar pieces, in prose and verse, copied in a round
youthful handwriting, and signed " Gray." Among them
a copy of elegiacs, on the 5th of November, struck me
as particularly clever, and it might be well, as the body
of Gray's works is so small, and his Latin verse so admirable, to include several of these in a complete edition
of his writings. They do not, however, greatly concern
us here.

As early as May 1736 it is curious to find the dulness
of Cambridge already lying with a leaden weight on the
nerves and energies of Gray, a youth scarcely in his
twentieth year. In his letters to West he strikes exactly
the same note that he harped upon ten years later to
Wharton, twenty years later to Mason, thirty years later
to Norton Nichols, and in his last months, with more
shrill insistence than ever, to Bonstetten. The cloud
sank early upon his spirits. He writes to West : " when

we meet it will be my greatest of pleasures to know what
you do, what you read, and how you spend your time,
and to tell you what I do not read, and how I do not,
&c., for almost all *the employment of my hours may be best
explained by negatives;* take my word and experience
upon it, doing nothing is a most amusing business; and
yet *neither something nor nothing gives me any pleasure.*
When you have seen one of my days, you have seen a
whole year of my life ; they go round and round like
the blind horse in the mill, only he has the satisfaction
of fancying he makes a progress and gets some ground ;
my eyes are open enough to see the same dull prospect,
and to know that having made four-and-twenty steps
more, I shall be just where I was." This is the real
Gray speaking to us for the first time, and after a few
more playful phrases, he turns again, and gives us another
phase of his character.   " You need not doubt, therefore,
of having a first row in the front box of my little heart,
and I believe you are not in danger of being crowded
there ; it is asking you to an old play, indeed, but you
will be candid enough to excuse the whole piece for the
sake of a few tolerable lines."   Many clever and delicate
boys think it effective to pose as victims to melancholy,
and the former of these passages would possess no importance if it were not for its relation to the poet's later
expressions.   He never henceforward habitually rose above
this deadly dulness of the spirits.   His melancholy was
passive and under control, not acute and rebellious, like
that of Cowper, but it was almost more enduring.   It is
probable that with judicious medical treatment it might
have been removed, or so far relieved as to be harmless.
But it was not the habit of men in the first half of the
eighteenth century to take any rational care of their

health. Men who lived in the country and did not hunt, took no exercise at all. The constitution of the generation was suffering from the mad frolics of the preceding age, and almost everybody had a touch of gout or scurvy. Nothing was more frequent than for men, in apparently robust health, to break down suddenly, at all points, in early middle life. People were not in the least surprised when men like Garth and Fenton died of mere indolence, because they had become prematurely corpulent and could not be persuaded to get out of bed. Gay, Thomson, and Gray are illustrious examples of the neglect of all hygienic precaution among quiet middle-class people in the early decades of the century. Gray took no exercise whatever; Cole reports that he said at the end of his life that he had never thrown his leg across the back of a horse, and this was really a very extraordinary confession for a man to make in those days. But we shall have to return to the subject of Gray's melancholy, and we need not dwell upon it here, further than to note that it began at least with his undergraduate days. He was considered effeminate at college, but the only proof of this that is given to us is one with which the most robust modern reader must sympathise, namely that he drank tea for breakfast, while all the rest of the university, except Horace Walpole, drank beer.

The letter from which we have just quoted goes on to show that the idleness of his life existed only in his imagination. He was, in fact, at this time wandering at will along the less-trodden paths of Latin literature, and rapidly laying the foundation of his unequalled acquaintance with the classics. He is now reading Statius, he tells West, and he encloses a translation of about one hundred and ten lines from the sixth book of the *Thebaid*.

This is the first example of his English verse which has
been preserved. It is very interesting, as showing already
the happy instinct which led Gray to reject the mode of
Pope in favour of the more massive and sonorous verse-
system of Dryden. He treats the heroic couplet with
great skill, but in close discipleship of the latter master in
his *Fables*. To a trained ear, after much study of minor
English verse written between 1720 and 1740, these
couplets have almost an archaic sound, so thoroughly are
they out of keeping with the glib, satiric poetry of the
period. Pope was a splendid artificer of verse, but there
was so much of pure intellect, and of personal temperament, in the conduct of his art, that he could not pass on
his secret to his pupils, and in the hands of his direct
imitators the heroic couplet lost every charm but that of
mere sparkling progress. The verse of such people as
Whitehead had become a simple voluntary upon knitting-
needles. Gray saw the necessity of bringing back
melody and volume to the heroic line, and very soon the
practice of the day disgusted him, as we shall see, with
the couplet altogether. For the present he was learning
the principles of his art at the feet of Dryden. West was
delighted with the translation, and compared Gray con-
tending with Statius to Apollo wrestling with Hyacinth.
In a less hyperbolical spirit, he pointed out, very justly,
the excellent rendering of that peculiarly Statian phrase,
Summos auro mansueverat ungues, by

And calm'd the terrors of his claws in gold.

We find from Walpole that Gray spent his vacations in
August, 1736, at his uncle's house at Burnham, in Buckinghamshire ; and here he was close to the scene of so
many of his later experiences, the sylvan parish of Stoke-

Pogis. For the present, however, all we hear is that he is too lazy to go over to Eton, which the enthusiastic Walpole and West consider to be perfectly unpardonable. A year later he is again with his uncle at Burnham ; and it is on this occasion that he discovers the since-famous beeches. He is writing to Horace Walpole, and he says :—

My Uncle is a great hunter in imagination ; his dogs take up every chair in the house, so I am forced to stand at the present writing ; and though the gout forbids him galloping after them in the field, yet he continues still to regale his ears and nose with their comfortable noise and stink. He holds me mighty cheap, I perceive, for walking when I should ride, and reading when I should hunt. My comfort amidst all this is, that I have at the distance of half a mile, through a green lane, a forest (the vulgar call it a common), all my own, at least, as good as so, for I spy no human thing in it but myself. It is a little chaos of mountains and precipices, mountains, it is true, that do not ascend much above the clouds, nor are the declivities quite so amazing as Dover Cliff ; but just such hills as people who love their necks as well as I do may venture to climb, and crags that give the eye as much pleasure as if they were more dangerous. Both vale and hill are covered with most venerable beeches, and other very reverend vegetables, that, like most other ancient people, are always dreaming out their old stories to the winds. At the foot of one of these squats ME (il penseroso) and there I grow to the trunk for a whole morning. The timorous hare and sportive squirrel gambol around me like Adam in Paradise before he had an Eve ; but I think he did not use to read Virgil, as I commonly do.

This is the first expression, as far as I am aware, of the modern feeling of the picturesque. We shall see that it became more and more a characteristic impulse with Gray as years went by. In this letter, too, we see that at the age of twenty-one he had already not a little of that sprightly wit and variety of manner which make him one of the most delightful letter-writers in any literature.

At Burnham, in 1737, he made the acquaintance of a very interesting waif of the preceding century. Thomas Southerne, the once famous author of *Oroonoko* and *The Fatal Marriage*, the last survivor of the age of Dryden, was visiting a gentleman in the neighbourhood of Burnham, and was so much pleased with young Gray, that though he was seventy-seven years of age he often came over to the house of Mr. Antrobus to see him. Still oftener, without doubt, the young poet went to see the veteran, whose successes on the stage of the Restoration took him back fifty years to a society very different from that in which he now vegetated on the ample fortune which his tragedies still brought him in. Unhappily his memory was almost entirely gone, though he lived nine years more, and died of sheer old age on the borders of ninety ; so that Gray's curiosity about Dryden and the other poets his friends was more provoked than gratified. However, Gray found him as agreeable an old man as could be, and liked " to look at him and think of *Isabella* and *Oroonoko*," those personages then still being typical of romantic disappointment and picturesque sensibility. About this time, moreover, we may just note in passing, died Matthew Green, whose posthumous poem of the *The Spleen* was to exercise a considerable influence over Gray, and to be one of the few contemporary poems which he was able fervidly to admire.

Lest, however, the boy should seem too serious and precocious, if we know him only by the scholarly letters to West, let us print here, for the first time, a note to his tutor, the Rev. George Birkett, Fellow of Peterhouse, a

C

note which throws an interesting light on his manners.
The postmark of this letter, which has lately been discovered at Pembroke College, is October 8, the year, I
think, 1736 :—

S^r,—As I shall stay only a fortnight longer in town, I'll beg
you to give yourself the trouble of writing out my Bills, and
sending 'em, that I may put myself out of your Debt, as soon as
I come down : if Piazza should come to you, you'll be so good
as to satisfie him : I protest, I forget what I owe him, but he is
honest enough to tell you right. My Father and Mother desire
me to send their compliments, and I beg you'd believe me
S^r, your most obed^t humble Servt
T. GRAY.

The amusing point is that the tutor seems to have flown
into a rage at the pert tone of this epistle, and we have
the rough draft of two replies on the fly-sheet. The first
addresses him as " pretty Mr. Gray," and is a moral box
on the ear ; but this has been cancelled, as wrath gave
way to discretion, and the final answer is very friendly,
and states that the writer would do anything "for your
father and your uncle, Mr. Antrobus (Thos.)." Signor
Piazza was the Italian master to the University, and six
months later we find Gray, and apparently Horace Walpole also, learning Italian " like any dragon." The course
of study habitual at the University was entirely out of
sympathy with Gray's instinctive movements after knowledge. He complains bitterly of having to endure lectures
daily and hourly, and of having to waste his time over
mathematics, where his teacher was the celebrated Professor Nicholas Saunderson, whose masterly *Elements of
Algebra*, afterwards the text-books of the University, were
still known only by oral tradition. For such learning
Gray had neither taste nor patience. " It is very pos-

sible," he writes to West, " that two and two make four, but I would not give four farthings to demonstrate this ever so clearly ; and if these be the profits of life, give me the amusements of it." His account of the low condition of classic learning at Cambridge we must take with a grain of salt. As an undergraduate he would of course see nothing of the great lights of the University, now sinking beneath the horizon ; such a shy lad as he would not be asked to share the conversation of Bentley, or Snape, or the venerable Master of Jesus. What does seem clear from his repeated denunciations of " that pretty collection of desolate animals " called Cambridge, is that classical taste was at a very low ebb among the junior fellows and the elder undergraduates. The age of the great Latinists had passed away ; the Greek revival, which Gray did much to start, had not begun, and 1737 was certainly a dull year at the University. It seems that there were no Greek text-books for the use of schools until 1741, and the method of pronouncing that language was as depraved as possible. A few hackneyed extracts from Homer and Hesiod were all that a youth was required to have read in order to pass his examination. Plato and Aristotle were almost unknown, and Gray himself seems to have been the only person at Cambridge who attempted seriously to write Greek verse. It is not difficult to understand that when, with the third term of his second year, his small opportunities of classical reading were taken from him, and he saw himself descend into the Cimmerian darkness of undiluted mathematics, the heart of the young poet sank within him. In December 1736 there was an attempt at rebellion ; he declined to take degrees, and announced his intention of quitting college, but as we hear no more of this, and as he stayed two years longer at Cambridge, we may believe that this was overruled.

Meanwhile the leaden rod seemed to rule the fate of the quadruple alliance. West grew worse and worse, hopelessly entangled in consumptive symptoms. Walpole lost his mother in August of 1737, and after this was a kind of waif and stray until he finally left England in 1739. Gray, whether in Cambridge or London, reverts more and more constantly to his melancholy. "Low spirits are my true and faithful companions ; they get up with me, go to bed with me, make journeys and returns as I do ; nay, and pay visits, and will even affect to be jocose, and force a feeble laugh with me ; but most commonly we sit together, and are the prettiest insipid company in the world. However, when you come," he writes to West, " I believe they must undergo the fate of all humble companions, and be discarded. Would I could turn them to the same use that you have done, and make an Apollo of them. If they could write such verses with me, not hartshorn, nor spirit of amber, nor all that furnishes the closet of the apothecary's wisdom, should persuade me to part with them." For West had been writing a touching eulogy *ad amicos*, in the manner of Tibullus, inspired by real feeling and a sad presentiment of the death that lay five years ahead. In reading these lines of Gray's, we hardly know whether most to admire the marvellous lightness and charm of the style, or to be concerned at such confession of want of spirits in a lad of twenty-one. His letters, however, when they could be wrung out of his apathy, were precious to poor West at Oxford ; " I find no physic comparable to your letters : prescribe to me, dear Gray, as often and as much as you think proper," and the amiable young pedants proceed, as before, to the

analysis of Poseidippos, and Lucretius, and such like frivolous reading.   One of West's letters contains a piece of
highly practical advice.   "Indulge, amabo te, plusquam
soles, corporis exercitationibus," but bodily exercise was
just what Gray declined to indulge in to the end of his
life.   He does not seem to have been even a walker; in-
doors he was a bookworm, and out-of-doors a saunterer and
a dreamer; nor was there ever, it would seem, a "good
friend Matthew" to urge the too-pensive student out into
the light of common life.

Certain interesting poetical exercises mark the close of
Gray's undergraduate career.   A Latin ode in Sapphics
and a fragment in Alcaics were sent in June, 1738, to
West, who had just left Oxford for the Inner Temple.
The second of these, which is so brief that it may surely
be quoted here,—

> O lacrymarum fons, tenero sacros
> Ducentium ortus ex animo; quater
>   Felix! in imo qui scatentem
>   Pectore te, pia Nympha, sensit,

has called forth high eulogy from scholars of every succeeding generation.   It is in such tiny seed-pearl of song
as this that we find the very quintessence of Gray's peculiar
grace and delicacy.   To July 1737 belongs a version
into English heroics of a long passage from Propertius,
beginning—

> Now prostrate, Bacchus, at thy shrine I bend,

which I have not met with in print; and another piece
from the same poet, beginning "Long as of youth,"
which occurs in all the editions of Gray, bears on the
original MS. at Pembroke the date Dec. 1738.   It

may be remarked that in the printed copies the two last
lines,—

> You whose young bosoms feel a nobler flame
> Redeem what Crassus lost and vindicate his name,

have accidentally dropped out.   In September 1738 Gray
left Cambridge, and took up his abode in his father's house
for six months, apparently with no definite plans regarding
his own future career ; but out of this sleepy condition of
mind he was suddenly waked by Horace Walpole's pro-
position that they should start together on the grand tour.
The offer was a generous one.   Walpole was to pay all
Gray's expenses, but Gray was to be absolutely independent : there was no talk of the poet's accompanying
his younger friend in any secondary capacity, and it is
only fair to Horace Walpole to state that he seems to have
acted in a thoroughly kind and gentlemanly spirit.   What
was still more remarkable was, that without letting Gray
know, he made out his will before starting, and so arranged
that had he died while abroad, Gray would have been his
sole legatee.   The frivolities of Horace Walpole have been
dissected with the most cruel frankness ; it is surely only
just to point out that in this instance he acted a very
gracious and affectionate part.   On the 29th of March,
1739, the two friends started from Dover.

CHAPTER II.

GRAY was only out of his native country once, but that single visit to the Continent lasted for nearly three years, and produced a very deep impression upon his character. It is difficult to realize what he would have become without this stimulus to the animal and external part of his nature. He was in danger of settling down in a species of moral inertia, of becoming dull and torpid, of spoiling a great poet to make a little pedant. The happy frivolities of France and Italy, though they were powerless over the deep springs of his being, stirred the surface of it, and made him bright and human. It is to be noticed that we hear nothing of his "true and faithful companion, melancholy," while he is away in the south ; he was cheerfully occupied, taken out of himself, and serene in the gaiety of others. The two friends enjoyed a very rough passage from Dover to Calais, and on landing Gray anticipated Dr. Johnson by being surprised that the inhabitants of the country could speak French so well. He also discovered that they were all " Papishes," and briskly adapted himself to the custom of the land by attending high mass the next day, which happened to be Easter Monday. In the afternoon the companions set out through a snow-storm for Boulogne in a post-chaise, a con-

veyance—not then imported into England—which filled
the young men with hilarious amazement.   Walpole, sensibly suggesting that there was no cause for hurry, refused to
be driven express to Paris; and so they loitered very agreeably through Picardy, stopping at Montreuil, Abbeville, and
Amiens.   From the latter city Gray wrote an amusing
account of his journey to his mother, containing a lively
description of French scenery.   "The country we have
passed through hitherto has been flat, open, but agreeably
diversified with villages, fields well cultivated, and little
rivers.   On every hillock is a windmill, a crucifix, or a
Virgin Mary dressed in flowers and a sarcenet robe; one
sees not many people or carriages on the road.   Now and
then indeed you meet a strolling friar, a countryman with
his great muff, or a woman riding astride on a little ass,
with short petticoats, and a great head-dress of blue wool."

On the 9th of April, rather late on a Saturday evening,
they rolled into Paris, and after a bewildering drive
drew up at last at the lodgings which had been prepared
for them, probably in or near the British Embassy, and
found themselves warmly welcomed by Walpole's cousins,
the Conways, and by Lord Holdernesse.   These young
men were already in the thick of the gay Parisian tumult,
and introduced Walpole, and Gray also as his friend, to
the best society.   The very day after their arrival they
dined at Lord Holdernesse's to meet the Abbé Prévôt-
d'Exiles, author of that masterpiece of passion, *Manon
Lescaut*, and now in his forty-second year.   It is very
much to be deplored that we do not possess in any form
Gray's impressions of the illustrious Frenchmen with whom
he came into habitual contact during the next two months.
He merely mentions the famous comic actress, Mademoiselle Jeanne Quinault "la Cadette," who was even

then, though in the flower of her years, coquettishly
threatening to leave the stage, and who did actually
retire, amid the regrets of a whole city, before Gray came
back to England. She reminded the young Englishman
of Mrs. Clive, the actress, but he says nothing of those
famous Sunday suppers at which she presided, and at
which all that was witty and brilliant in Paris was re-
hearsed or invented. These meetings, afterwards developed into the sessions of the Société du Bout du Banc,
were then only in their infancy; yet there, from his
corner unobserved, the little English poet must have
keenly noted many celebrities of the hour, whose laurels
were destined to wither when his were only beginning to
sprout. There would be found the "most cruel of amateurs," the Comte de Caylus ; Voisenon, still in the flush
of his reputation ; Moncrif, the lover of cats, with his
strange dog-face ; and there or elsewhere we know that
Gray met and admired that prince of frivolous ingenuities,
the redoubtable Marivaux. But of all this his letters
tell us nothing, nothing even of the most curious of his
friendships, that with Crébillon *fils*, who, according to
Walpole, was their constant companion during their stay
in Paris.

All the critics of Gray have found it necessary to
excuse or explain away that remarkable statement of his,
that " as the paradisaical pleasures of the Mahometans
consist in playing upon the flute, *etc.*, be mine to read
eternal new romances of Marivaux and Crébillon." Mason
considered this very whimsical, and later editors have
hoped that it meant nothing at all. But Gray was not a
man to say what he did not mean, even in jest. Such a
reasonable and unprejudiced mind as his may be credited
with a meaning, however paradoxical the statement it

makes. It is quite certain, from various remarks scattered through his correspondence, that the literature of the French regency, the boudoir poems and novels of the alcove, gave him more pleasure than any other form of contemporary literature. He uses language, in speaking of Gresset, the author of *Vert-Vert*, which contrasts curiously with his coldness towards Sterne and Collins. But above all, he delighted in Crébillon; hardly had he arrived in Paris, than he sent West the *Lettres de la Marquise M * * * au Comte de R * * *,* which had been published in 1732, but which the success of *Tanzaï et Néardané* had pushed into a new edition. The younger Crébillon at this time was in his thirty-second year, discreet, confidential, the friend of every one, the best company in Paris; half his time spent in wandering over the cheerful city that he loved so much, the other half given to literature in the company of that strange colossus, his father, the tragic poet, the writing-room of this odd couple being shared with a menagerie of cats and dogs and queer feathered folk. Always a serviceable creature, and perhaps even already possessed with something of that Anglomania which led him at last into a sort of morganatic marriage with British aristocracy, Crébillon evidently did all he could to make Walpole and Gray happy in Paris; no chaperon could be more fitting than he to a young Englishman desirous of threading the mazes of that rose-coloured Parisian Arcadia which had survived the days of the Regency, and had not yet ceased to look on Louis XV. as the Celadon of its pastoral valleys. It was a charming world of fancy and caprice; a world of milky clouds floating in an infinite azure, and bearing a mundane Venus to her throne on a Frenchified Cythera. And what strange figures were bound to the golden car ; generals, and abbés, and elderly academicians, laughing philosophers and weeping tragedians, a motley crew united in the universal *culte du Tendre*, gliding down a stream of elegance and cheerfulness and tolerance that was by no means wholly ignoble.

All this, but especially the elegance and the tolerance, made a deep impression upon the spirit of Gray. He came from a Puritan country ; and was himself, like so many of our greatest men, essentially a puritan at heart ; but he was too acute not to observe where English practice was unsatisfactory. Above all, he seems to have detected the English deficiency in style and grace ; a deficiency then, in 1739, far more marked than it had been half a century earlier. He could not but contrast the young English squire, that engaging and florid creature, with the bright, sarcastic, sympathetic companion of his walks in Paris, not without reflecting that the healthier English lad was almost sure to develop into a terrible type of fox-hunting stupidity in middle life. He, for one, then, and to the end of his days, would cast in his lot with what was refined and ingenious, and would temper the robustness of his race with a little Gallic brightness. Moreover his taste for the novels of Marivaux and Crébillon, with their ingenious analysis of emotion, their odour of musk and ambergris, their affectation of artless innocence, and their quick parry of wit, was not without excuse, in a man framed as Gray was for the more brilliant exercises of literature, and forced to feed, in his own country, if he must read romances at all, on the coarse rubbish of Mrs. Behn, or Mrs. Manley. Curiously enough at that very moment, Samuel Richardson was preparing for the press that excellent narrative of *Pamela* which was destined to found a great modern school of fiction in England, a

school which was soon to sweep into contempt and
oblivion all the "crébillonage-amarivaudé" which Gray
delighted in, a contempt so general that one stray reader
here or there can scarcely venture to confess that he still
finds the *Hasard au coin du Feu* very pleasant and
innocent reading. We shall have to refer once again to
this subject, when we reach the humorous poems in which
Gray introduced into English literature this rococo manner.

Gray became quite a little fop in Paris. He complains
that the French tailor has covered him with silk and
fringe, and has widened his figure with buckram, a yard
on either side. His waistcoat and breeches are so tight
that he can scarcely breathe ; he ties a vast solitaire
around his neck, wears ruffles at his fingers' ends, and
sticks his two arms into a muff. Thus made beautifully
genteel he and Walpole rolled in their coach to the
Comedy and the Opera, visited Versailles and the sights
of Paris, attended installations and spectacles, and saw
the best of all that was to be seen. Gray was absolutely
delighted with his new existence ; " I could entertain
myself this month," he wrote to West, " merely with the
common streets and the people in them ;" and Walpole,
who was good-nature itself during all this early part of the
tour, insisted on sending Gray out in his coach to see all
the collections of fine art, and other such sights as were
not congenial to himself, since Horace Walpole had not
yet learned to be a connoisseur. Gray occupied himself
no less with music, and his letters to West contain some
amusing criticisms of French opera. The performers, he
says, " come in and sing sentiment in lamentable strains,
neither air nor recitation ; only, to one's great joy, they
were every now and then interrupted by a dance, or, to
one's great sorrow, by a chorus that borders the stage from

one end to the other, and screams, past all power of
simile to represent. . . . .　Imagine, I say, all this trans-
acted by cracked voices, trilling divisions upon two notes-
and-a-half, accompanied by an orchestra of humstrums,
and a whole house more attentive than if Farinelli sung,
and you will almost have formed a just idea of the thing."
And, again, later, he writes " des miaulemens et des
heurlemens effroyables, melés avec un tintamarre du dia-
ble,—voilà la musique Françoise en abrégé."　At first
the weather was extremely bad, but in May they began
to enjoy the genial climate ; they took long excursions to
Versailles and Chantilly, happy " to walk by moonlight,
and hear the ladies and the nightingales sing."

On the 1st of June, in company with Henry Conway,
Walpole and Gray left Paris and settled at Rheims for
three exquisite summer months.　I fancy that these were
among the happiest weeks in Gray's life, the most sunny
and unconcerned.　As the three friends came with particular introductions from Lord Conway, who knew Rheims
well, they were welcomed with great cordiality into all
the best society of the town.　Gray found the provincial
assemblies very stately and graceful, but without the easy
familiarity of Parisian manners.　The mode of entertainment was uniform, beginning with cards, in the midst of
which every one rose to eat what was called the *gouter*, a
service of fruits, cream, sweetmeats, crawfish, and cheese.
People then sat down again to cards, until they had played
forty deals, when they broke up into little parties for a
promenade.　That this formality was sometimes set aside
we may gather from a very pretty little vignette that Gray
slips into a letter to his mother :—

The other evening we happened to be got together in a com-

pany of eighteen people, men and women of the best fashion
here, at a garden in the town, to walk, when one of the ladies
bethought herself of asking, Why should we not sup here?
Immediately the cloth was laid by the side of a fountain under
the trees, and a very elegant supper served up; after which another said, "Come, let us sing," and directly began herself.
From singing we insensibly fell to dancing, and singing in a
round; when somebody mentioned the violins, and immediately
a company of them was ordered, minuets were begun in the open
air, and then came country dances, which held till four o'clock
next morning; at which hour the gayest lady then proposed, that
such as were weary should get into their coaches, and the rest
of them should dance before them with the music in the van;
and in this manner we paraded through all the principal streets
of the city, and waked everybody in it. Mr. Walpole had a
mind to make a custom of the thing, and would have given a
ball in the same manner next week; but the women did not
come into it; so I believe it will drop, and they will return to
their dull cards and usual formalities.

Walpole intended to spend the winter of 1739 in the
South of France, and was therefore not unwilling to loiter
by the way. They thought to stay a fortnight at Rheims,
but they received a vague intimation that Lord Conway
and that prince of idle companions, the ever-sparkling
George Selwyn, were coming, and they hung on for three
months in expectation of them. At last, on the 7th of
September, they left Rheims, and entered Dijon three
days later. The capital of Burgundy, with its rich architecture and treasuries of art, made Gray regret the frivolous months they had spent at Rheims, while Walpole,
who was eager to set off, would only allow him three or
four days for exploration. On the 18th of September
they were at Lyons, and this town became their head-
quarters for the next six weeks. The junction of the

rivers has provoked a multitude of conceits, but none
perhaps so pretty as this of Gray's :—" The Rhone and
Saône are two people, who, though of tempers extremely
unlike, think fit to join hands here, and make a little
party to travel to the Mediterranean in company ; the
lady comes gliding along through the fruitful plains of
Burgundy, incredibili lenitate, ita ut oculis in utram
partem fluit judicari non possit ; the gentleman runs all
rough and roaring down from the mountains of Switzerland to meet her ; and with all her soft airs she likes him
never the worse ; she goes through the middle of the city
in state, and he passes incog. without the walls, but waits
for her a little below."

A fortnight later the friends set out on an excursion
across the mountains, that they might accompany Henry
Conway, who was now leaving them, as far as Geneva.
They took the longest road through Savoy, that they
might visit the Grande Chartreuse, which impressed
Gray very forcibly by the solitary grandeur of its
situation.   It was, however, not on this occasion, but
two years later, that he wrote his famous *Alcaic Ode* in
the album of the monastery.   The friends slept as the
guests of the fathers, and proceeded next day to Cham-
béry, which greatly disappointed them ; and sleeping
one night at Aix-les-Bains, which they found deserted,
and another at Annecy, they arrived at last at Geneva.
They stayed there a week, partly to see Conway settled,
and partly because they found it very bright and hospitable, returning at last to Lyons through the spurs of the
Jura, and across the plains of La Bresse.   They found
awaiting them a letter from Sir Robert Walpole, in which
he desired his son to go on to Italy, so they gladly
resigned their project of spending the winter in France

and pushed on at once to the foot of the Alps ; armed
against the cold with " muffs, hoods, and masks of beaver,
fur boots, and bearskins." On the 6th of November
they descended into Italy, after a very severe and painful
journey of a week's duration, through two days of which
they were hardly less frightened than Addison had been
during his Alpine adventures a generation earlier. It
was on the sixth day of this journey that the incident
occurred which was so graphically described both by
Gray and Walpole, and which is often referred to. Walpole had a fat little black spaniel, called Tory, which he
was very fond of ; and as this pampered creature was
trotting beside the ascending chaise, enjoying his little
constitutional, a young wolf sprang out of the covert and
snatched the shrieking favourite away from amongst the
carriages and servants before any one had the presence of
mind to draw a pistol. Walpole screamed and wept, but
Tory had disappeared for ever. Mason regrets that Gray
did not write a mock-heroic poem on this incident, as a
companion to the ode on Walpole's cat, and it must be
admitted that the theme was an excellent one.

The name of Addison has just been mentioned, and Walpole's remarks about the horrors of Alpine travelling do
indeed savour of the old-fashioned fear of what was sublime
in nature. But Gray's sentiments on the occasion were very
different, and his letter to his mother dilates on the beauty
of the crags and precipices in a way that shows him to have
been the first of the romantic lovers of nature, since even
Rousseau had then hardly developed his later and more
famous attitude, and Vernet had only just begun to con-
template the sea with ecstasy. On the 7th of November,
1739, the travellers had reached Turin, but among the
clean streets and formal avenues of that prosaic city, the

thoughts of Gray were still continually in the wonders he
had left behind him. In a delightful letter to West,
written nine days later, he is still dreaming of the Alps.
" I own I have not, as yet, anywhere met with those
grand and simple works of art that are to amaze one, and
whose sight one is to be the better for ; but those of
nature have astonished me beyond expression. In our
little journey up to the Grande Chartreuse I do not
remember to have gone ten paces without an exclamation
that there was no restraining ; *not a precipice, not a tor-
rent, not a cliff, but is pregnant with religion and poetry.*
There are certain scenes that would awe an atheist into
belief, without the help of other argument. One need
not have a very fantastic imagination to see spirits there
at noon-day. You have Death perpetually before your
eyes, only so far removed as to compose the mind without
frighting it. I am well persuaded St. Bruno was a man of
no common genius, to choose such a situation for his
retirement ; and perhaps I should have been a disciple of
his, had I been born in his time." It is hard to cease
quoting, all this letter being so new, and beautiful, and
suggestive ; but perhaps enough has been given to show
in what terms and on what occasion the picturesqueness of
Switzerland was first discovered. At the same time the
innovator concedes that Mont Cenis does perhaps abuse
its privilege of being frightful. Among the precipices
Gray read Livy, *Nives cœlo prope immistæ,* but when the
chaise drove down into the sunlit plains of Italy, he laid
that severe historian aside, and plunged into the pages of
Silius Italicus.

On the 18th of November they passed on to Genoa,
which Gray particularly describes as " a vast semicircular
basin, full of fine blue sea, and vessels of all sorts and

sizes, some sailing out, some coming in, and others at
anchor; and all round it palaces, and churches peeping
over one another's heads, gardens, and marble terraces full
of orange and cypress trees, fountains and trellis-works
covered with vines, which altogether compose the grandest
of theatres." The music in Italy was a feast to him, and
from this time we may date that careful study of Italian
music which occupied a great part of the ensuing year.
Ten days at Genoa left them deeply in love with it, and
loth to depart; but they wished to push on, and crossing
the mountains they found themselves within three days
at Piacenza, and so at Parma; out of which city they
were locked on a cold winter's night, and were only able
to gain admittance by an ingenious stratagem which
amused them very much, but which they have neglected
to record. They greatly enjoyed the Correggios in this
place, for Horace Walpole was now learning to be a connoisseur, and then they proceeded to Bologna, where they
spent twelve days in seeing the sights. They found it
very irksome to be without introductions, especially after
the hospitality which they had enjoyed in France, and
as it was winter they could only see, in Gray's words, the
skeleton of Italy. He was at least able to observe " very
public and scandalous doings between the vine and the
elm-trees, and how the olive-trees are shocked there-upon."
It is also particularly pleasant to learn that he himself was
" grown as fat as a hog;" he was, in fact, perfectly happy
and well, perhaps for the only time in his life.

They crossed the Apennines on the 15th of the month,
and descended through a winding-sheet of mist into the
streets of Florence, where Mr. Horace Mann's servant met
them at the gates, and conducted them to his house,
which, with a certain interval, was to be their home for

fifteen months.   Horace Mann was a dull letter-writer,
but he seems to have been a very engaging and unwearying
companion.   Gray, a man not easily pleased, pronounced
him "the best and most obliging person in the world."
He was then resident, and afterwards envoy extraordinary
at the Court of Tuscany, and retains a place in history as
the correspondent of Horace Walpole through nearly half
a century of undivided friendship.   Here again the travel-
stained youths had the pleasures of society offered to
them, and Gray could encase himself again in silk and
buckram, and wear ruffles at the tips of his fingers.
Moreover, his mind, the most actively acquisitive then
stirring in Europe, could engage once more in its enchanting exercises, and store up miscellaneous information
with unflagging zeal in a thousand nooks of brain and note-
book.   Music, painting, and statuary occupied him chiefly,
and his unpublished catalogues, not less strikingly than
his copious printed notes, show the care and assiduity of
his research.   His *Criticisms on Architecture and Painting
in Italy*, is not an amusing treatise, but it is without many
of the glaring faults of the æsthetic dissertations of the
age.   The remarks about antique sculpture are often very
just and penetrative, as fine sometimes as those exquisite
notes by Shelley, which first saw the light in 1880.   Some
of his views about modern masters, too, show the native
propriety of his taste, and his entire indifference to contemporary judgment.   For Caravaggio, for instance, then
at the height of his vogue, he has no patience ; although,
in common with all critics of the eighteenth century, and
all human beings till about a generation ago, he finds Guido
inexpressibly brilliant and harmonious.   It is, however,
chiefly interesting to us to notice that in these copious
notes on painting Gray distinguishes himself from other

writers of his time by his simple and purely artistic mode of considering what is presented to him, every other critic, as far as I remember, down to Lessing and Winckelmann, being chiefly occupied with rhetorical definitions of the action upon the human mind of art in the abstract. Gray scarcely mentions a single work, however, precedent to the age of Raphael ; and it will not do to insist too strongly upon his independence of the prejudices of his time.

In music he seems to have been still better occupied. He was astonished, during his stay in Florence, at the beauty and originality of the new school of Italian composers, at that time but little known in England. He seems to have been particularly struck with Leonardo da Vinci, who was then just dead, and with Bononcini and the German Hasse, who were still alive. At Naples a few months later he found Leonardo Leo, and was attracted by his genius. But the full ardour of his admiration was reserved for the works of G. B. Pergolesi, whose elevation above the other musicians of his age Gray was the first to observe and assert. Pergolesi, who had died four years before, at the age of twenty-six, was entirely unknown outside Tuscany ; and to the English poet belongs the praise, it is said, of being the first to bring a collection of his pieces to London, and to obtain for this great master a hearing in British concert-rooms. Gray was one of the few poets who have possessed not merely an ear for music, but considerable executive skill. Mason tells us that he enjoyed, probably at this very time, instruction on the harpsichord from the younger Scarlatti, but his main gift was for vocal music. He had a small, but very clear and pure voice, and was much admired for his singing in his youth, but during later years was so shy that Walpole "never could but once prevail on him to give a proof of it ; and then it was with so much pain to himself, that it gave Walpole no manner of pleasure." In after-years he had a harpsichord in his rooms at college, and continued to cultivate this sentimental sort of company in his long periods of solitude. Gray formed a valuable collection of MS. music while he was in Italy ; it consisted of nine large volumes, bound in vellum, and was enriched by a variety of notes in Gray's handwriting.

It was at Florence, on the 12th of March, 1740, that Gray took into his head to commence a correspondence with his old schoolfellow, Dr. Thomas Wharton ("my dear, dear Wharton, which is a ' dear ' more than I give anybody else "), who afterwards became fellow of Pembroke Hall, and one of Gray's staunchest and most sympathetic friends. To the biographer of the poet, moreover, the name of Wharton must be ever dear, since it was to him that the least reserved and most personal of all Gray's early letters were indited. This Dr. Wharton was a quiet, good man, with no particular genius or taste, but dowered with that delightful tact and sympathetic attraction which are the lode-star of irritable and weary genius. He was by a few months Gray's junior, and survived him three and twenty years, indolently intending, it is said, to the last, to collect his memories of his great friend, but dying in his eightieth year so suddenly as to be incapable of any preparation. In this his first letter to Wharton Gray mentions the death of Pope Clement XII., which had occurred about a month before, and states his intention to be at Rome in time to see the coronation of his successor, which however, as it happened, was delayed six months. So little however were Walpole and Gray prepared for this, that they set out in the middle of March 1740 in great fear lest they should be too late, and entered Rome

on the 31st of that month. They found the conclave of
cardinals sitting and like to sit; and they prepared themselves to enjoy Rome in the meanwhile. The magnificence
of the ancient city infinitely surpassed Gray's expectation,
but he found modern Rome and its inhabitants very con-
temptible and disgusting. There was no society among
the Roman nobles, who pushed parsimony to an extreme,
and showed not the least hospitality. "In short, child,"
(Walpole says to West, on the 16th of April,) "after sunset
one passes one's time here very ill; and if I did not wish for
you in the mornings, it would be no compliment to tell you
that I do in the evening." From Tivoli, a month later,
Gray writes West a very contemptuous description of the
artificial cascades and cliffs of the Duke of Modena's
palace-gardens there; but a few days afterwards at Alba
and Frascati, he was inspired in a gentler mood with the
Alcaic Ode to Favonius, beginning "Mater rosarum." Of
the same date is a letter laughing at West, who had made
some extremely classical allusions in his correspondence,
and who is indulged with local colour to his heart's
content.

I am to-day just returned from Alba, a good deal fatigued, for
you know (from Statius) that the Appian is somewhat tiresome.
We dined at Pompey's; he indeed was gone for a few days to
his Tusculan, but, by the care of his villicus, we made an admirable meal. We had the dugs of a pregnant sow, a peacock,
a dish of thrushes, a noble scarus just fresh from the Tyrrhene,
and some conchylia of the Lake, with garum sauce. For my part
I never ate better at Lucullus's table. We drank half-a-dozen
cyathi apiece of ancient Alban to Pholoë's health; and, after
bathing, and playing an hour at ball, we mounted our essedum
again, and proceeded up the mount to the temple. The priests
there entertained us with an account of a wonderful shower of
birds' eggs, that had fallen two days before, which had no sooner

touched the ground, but they were converted into gudgeons; as also that the night past, a dreadful voice had been heard out of the Adytum, which spoke Greek during a full half-hour, but nobody understood it. But quitting my Romanities, to your great joy and mine, let me tell you in plain English that we come from Albano.

Some entertainments Gray had at Rome. He mentions one ball at which he performed the part of the mouse at the party. The chief virtuosa of the hour, La Diamantina, played on the violin, and Giovannino and Pasquelini sang. All the secular grand monde of Rome was there, and there Gray, from the corner where he sat regaling himself with iced fruits, watched the object of his hearty disapproval, the English Pretender, " displaying his rueful length of person." Gray's hatred of the Stuarts was one of his few pronounced political sentiments, and while at Rome he could not resist making a contemptuous jest of them in a letter which he believed that James would open. He says, indeed, that all letters sent or received by English people in Rome were at that time read by the Pretender. In June, as the cardinals could not make up their minds, the young men decided to wait no longer, and proceeded southwards to Terracina, Capua, and Naples. On the 17th of June they visited the remains of Herculaneum, then only just exposed and identified, and before the end of the month they went back to Rome. There, still finding that no Pope was elected, and weary of the dreariness and formality of that great city, Walpole determined to return to Florence. They had now been absent from home and habitually thrown upon one another for entertainment during nearly fifteen months, and their friendship had hitherto shown no abatement. But they had arrived at that point of familiarity when a very little disagreement is sufficient to produce a quarrel. No such serious falling-out happened for nearly a year more, but we find Gray, whose note-books were inexhaustible, a little peevish at being forced to leave the treasures of Rome so soon. However, Florence was very enjoyable. They took up their abode once more in the house of Horace Mann, where they looked down into the Arno from their bed-room windows, and could resort at a moment's notice to the marble bridge, to hear music, eat iced fruits, and sup by moonlight. It is a place, Gray says, " excellent to employ all one's animal sensations in, but utterly contrary to one's rational powers. I have struck a medal upon my-self ; the device is thus O, and the motto *Nihilissimo*, which I take in the most concise manner to contain a full account of my person, sentiments, occupations, and late glorious successes. We get up at twelve o'clock, break-fast till three, dine till four, sleep till six, drink cooling liquors till eight, go to the bridge till ten, sup till two, and so sleep till twelve again."

In the midst of all this laziness, however, the business of literature recurred to his thoughts. He wrote some short things in Latin, then a fragment of sixty hexameter verses on the Gaurus, and then set about a very ambitious didactic epic *De Principiis Cogitandi.* It is a curious com-mentary on the small bulk of Gray's poetical productions to point out that this Latin poem, only two fragments of which were ever written, is considerably the longest of his writings in verse. As we now possess it, it was chiefly written in Florence during the summer of 1740 ; some passages were added at Stoke in 1742 ; but by that time Gray had de-termined, like other learned Cambridge poets, Spenser and Milton, to bend to the vulgar ear, and leave his Latin behind him. The *De Principiis Cogitandi* is now entirely neglected, and at no time attracted much curiosity; yet it is a notable production in its way. It was an attempt to crystallize the philosophy of Locke, for which Gray entertained the customary reverence of his age, in Lucretian hexameters. How the Soul begins to Know; by what primary Notions Mnemosyne opens her succession of thoughts, and her slender chain of ideas; how Reason contrives to augment her slow empire in the natural breast of man; and how anger, sorrow, fear and anxious care are implanted there, of these things he applies himself to sing; and do not thou disdain the singer, thou glory, thou unquestioned second luminary of the English race, thou unnamed spirit of John Locke. With the exception of one episode in which he compares the human mind in reverie to a Hamadryad who wanders in the woodland, and is startled to find herself mirrored in a pool, the plan of this poem left no scope for fancy or fine imagery; the theme is treated with a certain rhetorical dignity, but the poet has been so much occupied with the matter in hand, that his ideas have suffered some congestion. Nevertheless he is himself, and not Virgil or Ovid or Lucretius, and this alone is no small praise for a writer of modern Latin verse.

If the *De Principiis Cogitandi* had been published when it was written, it is probable that it would have won some measure of instant celebrity for its author, but the undiluted conclusions of Locke were no longer interesting in a second hand form in 1774, when they had already been subjected to the expansions of Hume and the criticisms of Leibnitz. Nor was Gray at all on the wave of philosophical thought; he seems no less indifferent to Berkeley's *Principles of Human Knowledge* than he is unaware of Hume's *Treatise of Human Nature*, which had been printed in 1739, soon after Gray left England. This Latin epic was a distinct false start, but he did not totally abandon the hope of completing it until 1746.

In August 1740 the friends went over to Bologna for a week, and on their return had the mortification to learn that a Pope, Benedict XIV., had been elected while they were within four days' journey of Rome. They began to think of home; there were talks of taking a felucca over from Leghorn to Marseilles, or of crossing through Germany by Venice and the Tyrol. Florence they began to find, "one of the dullest cities in Italy," and there is no doubt that they began to be on very strained and uncomfortable terms with one another. They had the grace, however, absolutely to conceal it from other people, and to the very last each of them wrote to West without the least hint of want of confidence in the other. On the 24th of April, 1741, Gray and Walpole set off from Florence, and spent a few days in Bologna to hear La Viscontina sing; from Bologna they proceeded to Reggio, and there occurred the famous quarrel which has perhaps been more often discussed than any other fact in Gray's life. It has been said that he discovered Walpole opening a letter addressed to Gray, or perhaps written by him, to see if anything unpleasant about himself were said in it, and that he broke away from him with scathing anger and scorn, casting Walpole off for ever, and at once continuing his journey to Venice alone. But this is really little more than conjecture. Both the friends were very careful to keep their counsel, and within three years the breach was healed. One thing is certain, that Walpole was the offender. When Gray was dead and Mason was writing his life, Walpole insisted that this fact should be stated, although he very reasonably declined to go into particulars for the public. He wrote a

little paragraph for Mason, taking the blame upon himself, but added for the biographer's private information a
longer and more intelligible account, saying that " while
one is living, it is not pleasant to read one's private
quarrels discussed in magazines and newspapers," but
desiring that Mason would preserve this particular
account, that it might be given to posterity. But Walpole lived on until 1797, and by a singular coincidence
Mason, who was so much younger, only survived him a
few days. Accordingly there was a delay in giving this
passage to the world, and though it is known to students
of Horace Walpole's *Correspondence*, it has never taken
the authoritative place it deserves in Gray's life. It is
all we possess in the way of direct evidence, and it does
great credit no less to Walpole's candour than to his
experience of the human heart. He wrote to Mason
(March 2, 1773) :—

I am conscious that in the beginning of the differences between
Gray and me the fault was mine. I was too young, too fond of
my own diversions, nay, I do not doubt, too much intoxicated
by indulgence, vanity, and the insolence of my situation as Prime
Minister's son, not to have been inattentive and insensible to the
feelings of one I thought below me; of one, I blush to say it,
that I knew was obliged to me; of one whom presumption and
folly, perhaps, made me deem not my superior *then* in parts,
though I have since felt my infinite inferiority to him. I treated
him insolently; he loved me, and I did not think he did. I
reproached him with the difference between us, when he acted
from convictions of knowing he was my superior. I often dis-
regarded his wishes of seeing places, which I would not quit
other amusements to visit, though I offered to send him to
them without me. Forgive me, if I say that his temper was
not conciliating; at the same time that I will confess to you
that he acted a more friendly part, had I had the sense to take

advantage of it, he freely told me of my faults. I declared I did
not desire to hear them, nor would correct them. You will not
wonder that with the dignity of his spirit, and the obstinate
carelessness of mine, the breach must have grown wider till we
became incompatible.

This is the last word on the subject of the quarrel,
and after a statement so generous, frank and lucid, it
only remains to remind the reader that these were lads
of twenty-three and twenty-four respectively, that they
had been thrown far too exclusively and too long on one
another for entertainment, and that probably Walpole is
too .hard upon himself in desiring to defend Gray.
There is not the slightest trace in his letters or in Gray's
of any rudeness on Walpole's part. The main point is
that the quarrel was made up in 1744, and that after
some coldness on Gray's side, they became as intimate
as ever for the remainder of their lives.

Walpole stayed at Reggio, and Gray's heart would
have stirred with remorse had he known that his old
friend was even then sickening for a quinsy, of which
he might have died, if the excellent Joseph Spence,
Oxford professor of Poetry and the friend of Pope, had
not happened to be passing through Reggio with Lord
Lincoln, and had not given up his whole time to nursing
him. Meanwhile the unconscious Gray, sore with pride,
passed on to Venice, where he spent two months, in the
company of a Mr. Whithead and a Mr. Chute. In July
he hired a courier, passed leisurely through the north of
Italy, visiting Padua and Verona, reached Turin on the
15th of August, and began to cross the Alps next day.
He stayed once more at the Grande Chartreuse, and inscribed in the Album of the Fathers his famous *Alcaic
Ode*, beginning " Oh Tu, severi Religio loci," which is

the best known and practically the last of his Latin
poems. In this little piece of twenty lines we first recognize that nicety of expression, that delicate lapidary
style, that touch of subdued romantic sentiment, which
distinguish the English poetry of Gray; while it is
perhaps not fantastic to detect in its closing lines the
first dawn of those ideas which he afterwards expanded
into the *Elegy in a Country Churchyard.* The original
MS. in the album became an object of great interest to
visitors to the hospice after Gray's death, and was highly
prized by the fathers. It exists, however, no longer; it
was destroyed by a rabble from Grenoble during the
French Revolution. Gray reached Lyons on the 25th of
August, and returned to London on the 1st of September, 1741, after an absence from England of exactly two
years and five months. Walpole, being cured of his
complaint, arrived in England ten days later. To a
good-natured letter from Henry Conway, suggesting a
renewal of intimacy between the friends, Gray returned
an answer of the coldest civility, and Horace Walpole
now disappears from our narrative for three years.

CHAPTER III.

ON his return from Italy Gray found his father lying very ill, exhausted by successive attacks of gout, and unable to rally from them. Two months later, on the 6th of November, 1741, he died in a paroxysm of the disease. His last act had been to squander his fortune, which seems to have remained until that time almost unimpaired, on building a country-house at Wanstead. Not only had he not written to tell his son of this adventure, but he had actually contrived to conceal it from his wife. Mason is not correct in saying that it became necessary to sell this house immediately after Philip Gray's death, or that it fetched 2000*l.* less than it had cost ; it remained in the possession of Mrs. Gray. With the ruins of a fortune Mrs. Gray and her sister, Mary Antrobus, seem to have kept house for a year in Cornhill, till, at the death of their brother-in-law, Mr. Jonathan Rogers, on the 21st of October, 1742, they joined their widowed sister Anna in her house at Stoke-Pogis, in Buckinghamshire. During these months they wound up their private business in Cornhill, and disposed of their shop on tolerably advantageous terms ; and apparently Gray first imagined that the family property would be enough to provide amply for him also. Accordingly he began the study of the law,

that being the profession for which he had been originally
intended.   For six months or more he seems to have
stayed in London, applying himself rather languidly to
common law, and giving his real thoughts and sympathies
to those who demanded them most, his mother and his
unfortunate friend Richard West.   The latter, indeed, he
found in a miserable condition ; in June 1740 that young
man, having lived at the Temple till he was sick of it,
left chambers, finding that neither the prestige of his
grandfather, nor the reputation of his uncle, Sir Thomas
Burnet, advanced him at all in their profession.   He was
without heart in his work, his talents were not drawn out
in the legal direction, and his affectionate and somewhat
feminine nature suffered from loneliness and want of congenial society.   He had hoped that Walpole would be
able to find him a post in the diplomatic service, or in
the army, but this was not possible.   Gray strongly disapproved of the step West took in leaving the Temple,
and wrote him from Florence a letter full of kindly and
cordial good sense ; but when he arrived in London he
found West in a far more broken condition of mind and
body than he had anticipated.   In extreme agitation
West confided to his friend a terrible secret which
he had discovered, and which Gray preserved in silence
until the close of his life, when he told it to Norton
Nicholls. · It is a painful story which need not be
repeated here, but which involved the reputation of
West's mother with the name of his late father's secretary, a Mr. Williams, whom she finally married when her
son was dead.   West had not the power to rally from
this shock, and the comfort of Gray's society only slightly
delayed the end.   In March 1742 he was obliged to
leave town, and went to stay with a friend at Popes,

near Hatfield, Herts, where he lingered three months, and died.

The winter which Gray and West spent together in London was remarkable in the career of the former as the beginning of his most prolific year of poetical composition, a vocal year to be followed by six of obstinate silence. The first original production in English verse was the fragment of a tragedy of *Agrippina*, of which one complete scene, and a few odd lines, have been preserved in his works. In this attempt at the drama he was inspired by Racine, and neither Addison, nor Aaron Hill, nor James Thomson, had contrived to be more cold or academic a playwright. The subject, which had been treated in tragedy more than a century earlier by May, was well adapted for stately stage-effect, and the scheme of Gray's play, so far as we know it, was not without interest. But he was totally unfitted to write for the boards, and even the beauty of versification in *Agrippina* cannot conceal from us for a moment its ineptitude. All that exists of the play is little else than a soliloquy in which the Empress defies the rage of Nero, and shows that she possesses

A heart that glows with the pure Julian fire,

by daring her son to the contest:

> Around thee call
> The gilded swarm that wantons in the sunshine
> Of thy full favour; Seneca be there
> In gorgeous phrase of laboured eloquence
> To dress thy plea, and Burrhus strengthen it
> With his plain soldier's oath, and honest seeming.
> Against thee—liberty and Agrippina!
> The world the prize! and fair befall the victors!

As a study in blank verse *Agrippina* shows the result of
long apprenticeship to the ancients, and marches with a
sharp and dignified step that reminds the reader more of
Landor than of any other dramatist.   In all other essen-
tials, however, the tragedy must be considered, like the
didactic epic, a false start ; but Gray was now very soon
to learn his real vocation.

The opening scene of the tragedy was sent down into
Hertfordshire to amuse West, who seemed at first to have
recovered his spirits, and who sat " purring by the fireside,
in his arm-chair, with no small satisfaction."   He was
able to busy himself with literature, delighting in the
new book of the *Dunciad*, and reading Tacitus for the
first time.   His cool reception of the latter roused Gray
to defend his favourite historian with great vigour.
" Pray do not imagine," he says, " that Tacitus, of all
authors in the world, can be tedious . . . . Yet what I
admire in him above all is his detestation of tyranny, and
the high spirit of liberty that every now and then breaks
out, as it were, whether he would or no."   Poor West
on the 4th of April, racked by an " importunissima
tussis," declines to do battle against Tacitus, but attacks
Agrippina with a frankness and a critical sagacity which
slew that ill-starred tragedy on the spot.   It is evident
that Gray had no idea of West's serious condition, for he
rallies him on being the first who ever made a muse of a
cough, and is confident that " those wicked remains of
your illness will soon give way to warm weather and
gentle exercise."   It is in the same letter that Gray speaks
with some coldness of *Joseph Andrews,* and reverts with
the warmth on which we have already commented to the
much more congenial romances of Marivaux and Crébillon.
We may here confess that Gray certainly misses, in com-

E

mon with most men of his time, the one great charm of
the literary character at its best, namely enthusiasm for
excellence in contemporaries. It is a sign of a dry age
when the principal authors of a country look askance on
one another. Some silly critics in our own days have
discovered with indignant horror the existence of "mutual
admiration societies." A little more acquaintance with
the history of literature might have shown them how
strong the sentiment of comradeship has been in every
age of real intellectual vitality. It is much to be deplored
that the chilly air of the eighteenth century prevented the "mutual admiration" of such men as Gray
and Fielding.

This is perhaps an appropriate point at which to pause
and consider the condition of English poetry at the
moment at which we have now arrived. When Gray
began seriously to write, in 1742, the considerable poets
then alive in England might have been counted on the
fingers of two hands. Pope and Swift were nearing the
close of their careers of glory and suffering, the former
still vocal to the last, and now quite unrivalled by any
predecessor in personal prestige. As a matter of fact,
however, he was not destined to publish anything more
of any consequence. Three other names, Goldsmith,
Churchill, and Cowper, were those of children not to
appear in literature for many years to come. Gray's
actual competitors, therefore, were only four in number.
Of these the eldest, Young, was just beginning to publish,
at the age of fifty-eight, the only work by which he is
now much remembered, or which can still be read with
pleasure. The *Night Thoughts* was destined to make
his the most prominent poetical figure for the next ten
years. Thomson, on the other hand, a younger and far

more vital spirit, had practically retreated already upon
his laurels, and was presently to die, without again
addressing the public except in the luckless tragedy of
Sophonisba, bequeathing, however, to posterity the treasure of his *Castle of Indolence*. Samuel Johnson had
published *London*, a nine days' wonder, and had subsided
into temporary oblivion. Collins, just twenty-one years
of age, had brought out a pamphlet of *Persian Eclogues*
without attracting the smallest notice from anybody.
Among the lesser stars, Allan Ramsay and Ambrose
Philips were retired old men, now a long while silent,
who remembered the days of Addison; Armstrong had
flashed into unenviable distinction with a poem more
clever than decorous; Dyer, one of the lazy men who
grew fat too soon, was buried in his own *Fleece ;* Shenstone and Akenside, much younger men, were beginning
to be talked about in the circle of their friends, but had
as yet done little. The stage, therefore, upon which
Gray proceeded very gingerly to step, was not a crowded
one, and before he actually ventured to appear in print,
it was stripped of its most notable adornments. Yet this
apparent advantage was in reality a great disadvantage ;
as Mr. Matthew Arnold admirably says, " born in the
same year with Milton, Gray would have been another
man ; born in the same year with Burns, he would have
been another man." As it was, his genius pined away
for want of movement in the atmosphere ; the wells of
poetry were stagnant, and there was no angel to strike
the waters.

The amiable dispute as to the merits of *Agrippina*
led the friends on to a wider theme, the peculiar qualities
of the style of Shakespeare. How low the standard of
criticism had fallen in that generation, may be estimated

when we consider that Theobald, himself the editor and
annotator of Shakespeare, in palming off his forgery of
The Double Falsehood, which contains such writing as
this,—

> Fond Echo, forego the light strain,
>   And heedfully hear a lost Maid;
> Go tell the false ear of the Swain
>   How deeply his vows have betrayed,

as a genuine work by the author of *Hamlet*, had ventured
to appeal to the style as giving the best evidence of the
truth of his pretensions.   Gray had a more delicate sense
of literary flavour than this, and his remarks about the
vigour and pictorial richness of Elizabethan drama, since
which " our language has greatly degenerated," are highly
interesting even to a modern reader.   Through April and
May he kept up a brisk correspondence, chiefly on books,
with West at Popes, and on the 5th of the latter month
he received from his friend an *Ode to May*, beginning

> Dear Gray, that always in my heart
> Possessest still the better part,

which is decidedly the most finished of West's productions.   Some of the stanzas of this ode possess much
suavity and grace :—

> Awake, in all thy glories drest,
> Recall the zephyrs from the west;
> Restore the sun, revive the skies,
> At mine and Nature's call, arise!
> Great Nature's self upbraids thy stay
> And misses her accustomed May.

This is almost in the later style of Gray himself, and
the poem received from him commendation as being

" light and genteel," a phrase that sounds curiously old-
fashioned nowadays.   Gray meanwhile is busy translating
Propertius, and shows no sign of application to legal
studies.   On the contrary, he has spent the month of
April in studying the *Peloponnesian War*, the greater
part of Pliny and Martial, Anacreon, Petrarch and
Aulus Gellius, a range of reading which must have
entirely excluded Coke upon Lyttelton.   West's last
letter is dated May 11, 1742, and is very cheerfully
written, but closes with words that afterwards took a
solemn meaning, " Vale, et vive paulisper cum vivis."
On the 27th of the same month Gray wrote a very long
letter to West, in which he shows no consciousness whatever of his friend's desperate condition ; this epistle contains an interesting reference to his own health :—

Mine, you are to know, is a white Melancholy, or rather
Leucocholy, for the most part ; which, though it seldom laughs
or dances, nor ever amounts to what one calls Joy or Pleasure,
yet is a good easy sort of a state, and *ça ne laisse que de s'amuser.*
The only fault is its vapidity, which is apt now and then to give
a sort of *Ennui*, which makes one form certain little wishes that
signify nothing.   But there is another sort, black indeed, which
I have now and then felt, that has somewhat in it like Tertul-
lian's rule of faith, *Credo quia impossibile est;* for it believes,
nay, is sure of everything that is unlikely, so it be but frightful; and on the other hand excludes and shuts its eyes to the
most possible hopes, and everything that is pleasurable; from
this the Lord deliver us ! for none but He and sunshiny weather
can do it.

Grimly enough, while he was thus analysing his feelings, his friend lay at the point of death.   Five days
after this letter was written West breathed his last, on
the 1st of June, 1742, in the twenty-sixth year of his
age, and was buried in the chancel of Hatfield Church.

Probably on the same day that West died, Gray went down into Buckinghamshire to visit his uncle and aunt Rogers at Stoke-Pogis, a village which his name has immortalized, and of which it may now be convenient to say a few words. The manor of Stoke Pogis or Poges is first mentioned in a deed of 1291, and passed through the hands of a variety of eminent personages down to the great Earl of Huntingdon in the reign of Henry VIII. The village, if such it can be called, is sparsely scattered over a wide extent of country. The church, a very picturesque structure of the fourteenth century, with a wooden spire, is believed to have been built by Sir John Molines about 1340. It stands on a little level space about four miles north of the Thames at Eton. From the neighbourhood of the church no vestige of hamlet or village is visible, and the aspect of the place is slightly artificial, like a rustic church in a park on the stage. The traveller almost expects to see the grateful peasantry of an opera, cheerfully habited, make their appearance, dancing on the greensward. As he faces the church from the south, the white building, extravagantly Palladian, which lies across the meadows on his left hand, is Stoke Park, begun under the direction of Alexander Nasmyth, the landscape-painter, in 1789, and finished by James Wyatt, R.A., for the Hon. Thomas Penn, who bought the manor from the representatives of Gray's friend Lady Cobham. At the back of the visitor, stands a heavy and hideous mausoleum, bearing a eulogistic inscription to Gray, and this also is due to the taste of Wyatt and was erected in 1799. If we still remain on the south side of the churchyard, the chimneys seen through the thick umbrageous foliage on our right hand, and behind the church, are those of the ancient Manor House, celebrated

by Gray in the *Long Story*, and built by the Earl of
Huntingdon in 1555. The road from Farnham Royal
passes close to it, but there is little to be seen. Although
in Gray's time it seems to have been in perfect preserva-
tion as an exquisite specimen of Tudor architecture, with
its high gables, projecting windows and stacks of clustered
chimney-shafts, it did not suit the corrupt Georgian taste
of the Penns, and was pulled down in 1789. Wyatt
refused to have anything to say to it, and remarked that
" the style of the edifice was deficient in those excellen-
cies which might have pleaded for restoration." Of the
historical building in which Sir Christopher Hatton lived
and Sir Edward Coke died nothing is left but the fantastic chimneys, and a rough shell which is used as a
stable. This latter was for some time fitted up as a
studio for Sir Edwin Landseer, and he was working here
in 1852, when he suddenly became deranged. This old
ruin, so full of memories, is only one of a number of
ancient and curious buildings within the boundaries of
the parish of Stoke Pogis. When Gray came to Stoke
in 1742, the Manor House was inhabited by the ranger
of Windsor Forest, Viscount Cobham, who died in 1749.
It was his widow who, as we shall presently see, became
the intimate friend of Gray and inspired his remarkable
poem of the *Long Story*.

The house of Mrs Rogers, to which Gray and his
mother now proceeded, was situated at West End, in the
northern part of the parish. It was reached from the
church by a path across the meadows, alongside the
hospital, a fine brick building of the sixteenth century,
and so by the lane leading out into Stoke Common. Just
at the end of this lane, on the left-hand side, looking
southwards, with the common at its back, stood West

End House, a simple farmstead of two stories, with a
rustic porch before the front door, and this was Gray's
home for many years.   It is now thoroughly altered and
enlarged, and no longer contains any mark of its original
simplicity.   The charm of the house to the poet must
have been that Burnham Beeches, Stoke Common, and
Brockhurst Woods, were all at hand, and within reach
of the most indolent of pedestrians.

Gray had been resident but very few days at Stoke-Pogis
before he wrote the poem with which his poetical works
usually open, his *Ode to Spring.*   Among the MS. at
Pembroke there occurs a copy of this poem, in Gray's
handwriting, entitled *Noon-Tide: an Ode;* and in the
margin of it there is found this interesting note: "The
beginning of June, 1742, sent to Fav: not knowing
he was then dead."   Favonius was the familiar name of
West, and this shows that Gray received no intimation of
his friend's approaching end, and no summons to his bed-
side.   The loss of West was one of the most profound
that his reserved nature ever suffered ; when that name
was mentioned to him, nearly thirty years afterwards, he
became visibly agitated, and to the end of his life he
seemed to feel in the death of West "the affliction of a
recent loss."   We are therefore not surprised to find the
Ode to Spring, which belongs to a previous condition of
things, lighter in tone, colder in sentiment, and more
trivial in conception than his other serious productions.
We are annoyed that, in the very outset, he should borrow
from Milton his " rosy-bosomed Hours," and from Pope
his "purple year."   Again there is a perplexing change of
tone from the beginning where he was perhaps inspired
by that exquisite strain of florid fancy, the *Pervigilium
Veneris*, to the stoic moralizings of the later stanzas :—

> How vain the ardour of the crowd,
> How low, how little are the proud,
> How indigent the great!

It may be noted, by the way, that for many years the last two adjectives, now so happily placed, were awkwardly transposed. The best stanza, without doubt, is the penultimate :—

> To Contemplation's sober eye
> Such is the race of Man :
> And they that creep and they that fly
> Shall end where they began.
> Alike the Busy and the Gay
> But flutter through life's little day,
> In Fortune's varying colours drest :
> Brush'd by the hand of rough Mischance
> Or chill'd by Age, their airy dance
> They leave, in dust to rest.

The final stanza, with its "glittering female," and its "painted plumage" is puerile in its attempted excess of simplicity, and errs, though in more fantastic language, exactly as such crude studies of Wordsworth's as *Andrew Jones* or *The Two Thieves* erred half a century later. Nothing was gained by the poet's describing himself "a solitary fly" without a hive to go to. The mistake was one which Gray never repeated, but it is curious to find two of the most sublime poets in our language, both specially eminent for loftiness of idea, beginning by eschewing all reasonable dignity of expression.

But although the *Ode to Spring* no longer forms a favourite part of Gray's poetical works, it possessed considerable significance in 1742, and particularly on account of its form. It was the first note of protest against the hard versification which had reigned in England for more

than sixty years. The Augustan age seems to have
suffered from a dulness of ear, which did not permit it to
detect a rhyme unless it rang at the close of the very next
pause. Hence, in the rare cases where a lyric movement
was employed, the ordinary octosyllabic couplet took the
place of those versatile measures in which the Elizabethan
and Jacobite poets had delighted, Swift, Lady Winchil-
sea, Parnell, Philips, and Green, the five poets of the
beginning of the eighteenth century who rebelled against
heroic verse, got no further in metrical innovation than
the shorter and more ambling couplet. Dyer, in his
greatly overrated piece called *Grongar Hill*, followed these
his predecessors. But Gray, from the very first, showed a
disposition to return to more national forms, and to work
out his stanzas on a more harmonic principle. He seems
to have disliked the facility of the couplet, and the vague
length to which it might be repeated. His view of a
poem was that it should have a vertebrate form, which
should respond, if not absolutely to its subject, at least to
its mood. In short he was a genuine lyrist, and our
literature had possessed none since Milton and the last
cavalier song-writers. Yet his stanzas are built up from
very simple materials. Here, in the *Ode to Spring*, we
begin with a quatrain of the common ballad-measures ;
an octosyllabic couplet is added, and this would close it
with a rustic effect, were the music not prolonged by the
addition of three lines more, while the stanza closes
gravely with a short line of six syllables.

The news of the death of West deepened Gray's vein
of poetry, but did not stop its flow. He poured forth his
grief and affection in some impassioned hexameters, full
of earnest feeling, which he afterwards tried, ineptly
enough, to tack on to the icy periods of his *De Principiis*

Cogitandi. In no other of his writings does Gray employ quite the same personal and emotional accents, in none does he speak out so plainly from the heart, and with so little attention to his singing robes :—

> Vidi egomet duro graviter concussa dolore
> Pectora, in alterius non unquam lenta dolorem ;
> Et languere oculos vidi, et pallescere amantem
> Vultum, quo nunquam Pietas nisi rara, Fidesque,
> Altus amor Veri, et purum spirabat Honestum.
> Visa tamen tardi demum inclementia morbi
> Cessere est, reducemque iterum roseo ore Salutem
> Speravi, atque una tecum, dilecte Favoni !
> Credulus heu longos, ut quondam, fallere Soles.

This fragment, the most attractive of his Latin poems, trips on a tag from Propertius, and suddenly ceases, nor is there extant any later effusion of Gray's in the same language. He celebrated the death of Favonius in another piece, which is far more familiar to general readers. The MS. of this sonnet, now at Cambridge, is marked " at Stoke : Aug. 1742 ;" it was not published till Mason included it in his Memoirs.

> In vain to me the smiling mornings shine.
>   And reddening Phœbus lifts his golden fire :
> The birds in vain their amorous descant join,
>   Or cheerful fields resume their green attire :
> These ears alas ! for other notes repine,
>   A different object do these eyes require ;
> My lonely anguish melts no heart but mine,
>   And in my breast th' imperfect joys expire.
> Yet morning smiles the busy race to cheer,
>   And new-born pleasure brings to happier men ;
> The fields to all their wonted tribute bear ;
>   To warm their little loves the birds complain ;
> I fruitless mourn to him that cannot hear,
>   And weep the more, because I weep in vain.

This little composition has suffered a sort of notoriety

from the fact that Wordsworth, in 1800, selected it as an
example of the errors of an ornate style, doing so because,
as he frankly admitted, "Gray stands at the head of those
who by their reasonings have attempted to widen the
space of separation betwixt Prose and Metrical composition, and was more than any other man curiously elaborate
in the structure of his own poetic diction." Wordsworth
declares that out of the fourteen lines of this poem only
five are of any value, namely the sixth, seventh, eighth,
thirteenth, and fourteenth, the language of which "differs
in no respect from that of prose." But this does not
appear to be particularly ingenuous. If we allow the sun
to be called Phœbus, and if we·pardon the "green attire,"
there is not a single expression in the sonnet which is
fantastic or pompous. It is simplicity itself in comparison
with most of Milton's sonnets, and it seems as though
Wordsworth might have found an instance of fatuous
grandiloquence much fitter to his hand in Young, or better
still in Armstrong, master of those who go about to call a
hat a "swart sombrero." Gray's graceful sonnet was
plainly the result of his late study of Petrarch, and we
may remind ourselves, in this age of flourishing sonneteers,
that it is almost the only specimen of its class that had
been written in English for a hundred years, certainly the
only one that is still read with pleasure. One other fact
may be noted, that in this little poem Gray first begins to
practise the quatrain of alternate heroics, which later on
became, as we shall see, the basis of all his harmonic
effects, and which he learned to fashion with more skill
than any other poet before or since.

In the same month of August was written the *Ode on a
Distant Prospect of Eton College*, or, as in Gray's own MS.
which I have examined, of *Eton College, Windsor, and the*

adjacent country. East and west from the church of
Stoke-Pogis, towards Stoke Green in the one direction
and towards Farnham Royal in the other, there rises a
gentle acclivity, from which the ground gradually slopes
southward to the Thames, and which lies opposite those
"distant spires" and "antique towers" which Gray has
sung in melodious numbers. The woodland parish of
Stoke is full of little rights-of-way, meadow-paths without
hedges, that skirt the breast of the ridge I speak of, and
reveal against the southern sky the embattled outline of
Windsor. The *Eton Ode* is redolent of Stoke-Pogis, and
to have sauntered where Gray himself must have muttered
his verses as they took shape, gives the reader a certain
sense of confidence in the poet's sincerity. Gray had of
late been much exercised about Eton; to see a place so
full of reminiscences, and yet be too distant to have
news of it, this was provoking to his fancy. In his last
letter to West he starts the reflection that he developed a
few months later in the *Ode.* It puzzled him to think
that Lord Sandwich and Lord Halifax, whom he could
remember as "dirty boys playing at cricket," were now
statesmen, while, "as for me, I am never a bit the
older, nor the bigger, nor the wiser than I was then, no,
not for having been beyond the sea." Lord Sandwich,
of course, as all readers of lampoons remember, remained
Gray's pet aversion to the end of his life, the type to him
of the man who, without manners, or parts, or character,
could force his way into power by the sheer insolence of
wealth. The *Eton Ode* was inspired by the regret that
the illusions of boyhood, the innocence that comes not of
virtue but of inexperience, the sweetness born not of a
good heart but of a good digestion, the elation which
childish spirits give and which owes nothing to anger or

dissipation, that these simple qualities cannot be preserved through life. Gray was, or thought he was, " never a bit the older " than he was at Eton, and it seemed to him that the world would be better if Lord Sandwich could have been kept for ever in the same infantile simplicity. This description of the joyous innocence of boyhood, a theme requiring indeed the optimism of a Pangloss, has never been surpassed as an *ex parte* statement on the roseate and ideal side of the question ; that the view of ethics is quite elementary, and would have done honour to the experience and science of one of Gray's good old aunts, detracts in no sense from the positive beauty of the poem as a strain of reflection ; and it has enjoyed a popularity with successive generations which puts it almost outside the pale of verbal criticism. When a short ode of one hundred lines has enriched our language with at least three phrases which have become part and parcel of our daily speech, it may be taken for granted that it is very admirably worded. Indeed the *Eton Ode* is one of those poems which have suffered from a continued excess of popularity, and its famous felicities, "to snatch a fearful joy," "regardless of their doom, the little victims play," " where ignorance is bliss, 'tis folly to be wise," have suffered the extreme degradation as well as the loftiest honour which attends on passages of national verse, since they have been so universally extolled that they have finally become commonplace witticisms to the million. It is well to take the stanza in which such a phrase occurs, and read it anew, with a determination to forget that one of its lines has been almost effaced in vulgar traffic :—

> While some on earnest business bent
>   Their murmuring labours ply
> 'Gainst graver hours that bring constraint
>   To sweeten liberty,

Some bold adventurers disdain
The limits of their little reign,
  And unknown regions dare descry;
Still as they run they look behind,
They hear a voice in every wind,
  And snatch a fearful joy.

It is only in the second stanza of the *Eton Ode* that
Gray permits himself to refer to the constant pressure of
regret for his lost friend; the fields are beloved in vain,
and in Wordsworth's exquisite phrase, he turns to share
the rapture,—ah! with whom? In yet one other poem
composed during this prolific month of August 1742, that
regret serves simply to throw a veil of serious and pathetic
sentiment over the tone of the reflection. The *Ode on
Adversity*, so named by Gray himself and by his first
editor Mason, but since styled, I know not why, the
Hymn to Adversity, is remarkable as the first of Gray's
poems in which he shows that stateliness of movement
and pomp of allegorical illustration which give an indi-
viduality in his mature style. No English poet, except
perhaps Milton and Shelley, has maintained the same
severe elevation throughout a long lyrical piece; perhaps
the fragments of such lyrists as Simonides gave Gray the
hint of this pure and cold manner of writing. The
shadowy personages of allegory throng around us, and we
are not certain that we distinguish them from one another.
The indifferent critic may be supposed to ask, which is
Prosperity and which is Folly, and how am I to distinguish them from the Summer Friend and from Thoughtless Joy? Adversity herself is an abstraction which has
few terrors and few allurements for us, and in listening to
the address made to her by the poet, we are apt to forget
her in our appreciation of the balanced rhythm and rich
persuasive sound :—

Wisdom in sable garb arrayed,
　Immersed in rapt'rous thought profound,
And Melancholy, silent maid,
　With leaden eye that loves the ground,
Still on thy solemn steps attend;
Warm Charity, the general friend,
　With Justice, to herself severe,
And Pity, dropping soft the sadly-pleasing tear.

O gently on thy suppliant's head,
　Dread goddess, lay thy chast'ning hand !
Not in thy Gorgon terrors clad,
　Not circled with the vengeful band
(As by the impious thou art seen)
With thund'ring voice, and threat'ning mien,
　With screaming Horror's funeral cry,
Despair, and fell Disease, and ghastly Poverty.

Thy form benign, O Goddess, wear,
　Thy milder influence impart,
Thy philosophic train be there,
　To soften, not to wound, my heart.
The gen'rous spark extinct revive,
Teach me to love, and to forgive,
　Exact my own defects to scan,
What others are to feel, and know myself a Man.

This last stanza, where he gets free from the allegorical
personages, is undoubtedly the best; and the curious
couplet about the "generous spark" seems to me to be
probably a reference to the quarrel with Walpole. If
this be thought fantastic, it must be remembered that
Gray's circle of experience and emotion was unusually
narrow. To return to the treatment of allegory and the
peculiar style of this ode, we are confronted by the
curious fact that it seems impossible to claim for these
qualities, hitherto unobserved in English poetry, precedency
in either Gray or Collins. Actual priority, of course,
belongs to Gray, for Collins wrote nothing of a serious

nature till 1745 or 1746 ; but his *Odes*, though so similar.
or rather so analogous, to Gray's, that every critic has
considered them as holding a distinct place together in
literature, were certainly not in any way inspired by Gray.
The latter published nothing till 1747, whereas in December, 1746, Collins' precious little volume saw the light.

It is difficult to believe that Collins, at school at
Winchester until 1741, at college at Oxford until 1744,
could have seen any of Gray's verses, which had not
then begun to circulate in MS., in the way in which
long afterwards the *Elegy* and the *Bard* passed from
eager hand to hand. We shall see that Gray read Collins
eventually, but without interest, while Collins does not
appear to have been ever conscious of Gray's existence ;
there was no mutual magnetic attraction between the two
poets, and we must suppose their extraordinary kinship
to have been a mere accident, the result of certain forces
acting simultaneously on more or less similar intellectual
compounds. There was no other resemblance between them,
as men, than this one gift of clear, pure, Simonidean song.
Collins was simply a reed, cut short and notched by the
great god Pan, for the production of enchanting flute-
melodies at intervals ; but for all other human purposes a
vain and empty thing indeed. In Gray the song, important
as it was, seemed merely one phase of a deep and consistent
character, of a brain almost universally accomplished, of
a man, in short, and not of a mere musical instrument.

One more work of great importance was begun at
Stoke in the autumn of 1742, the *Elegy wrote in a
Country Church-Yard*. It is, unfortunately, impossible
to say what form it originally took, or what lines or
thoughts now existing in it are part of the original
scheme. We shall examine this poem at length when we

F

reach the period of Gray's career to which it belongs in
its completed form ; but as the question is often asked,
and vaguely answered, where was the *Elegy* written, it
may at once be said that it was begun at Stoke in
October or November 1742, continued at Stoke immediately after the funeral of Gray's aunt, Miss Mary
Antrobus, in November 1749, and finished at Cambridge
in June 1750.   And it may here be remarked as a very
singular fact that the death of a valued friend seems to
have been the stimulus of greatest efficacy in rousing
Gray to the composition of poetry, and did in fact excite
him to the completion of most of his important poems.
He was a man who had a very slender hold on life himself, who walked habitually in the Valley of the Shadow
of Death, and whose periods of greatest vitality were
those in which bereavement proved to him, that, melancholy as he was, even he had something to lose and to
regret.

It is therefore perhaps more than a strong impression
that makes me conjecture the beginning of the *Elegy
wrote in a Country Church-Yard* to date from the funeral
of Gray's uncle, Jonathan Rogers, who died at Stoke-
Pogis on the 21st of October, 1742, and who was buried
with the Antrobus family in the church of the neighbouring parish of Burnham.   An ingenious Latin inscription
to him, in a marble tablet in the church of that name,
has always been ascribed to Gray himself.   Rogers died
at the age of sixty-five, having spent thirty-two years in
undisturbed felicity with his wife, born Anna Antrobus,
who survived him till near the end of her celebrated
nephew's life.   The death of Mr. Rogers completely
altered Gray's prospects.   Mrs. Rogers appears to have
been left with a very small fortune, just enough to sup-

port her and her sisters Mrs. Gray and Miss Antrobus, in genteel comfort, if they shared a house together, and had no extraneous expenses. The ladies from Cornhill accordingly came down to West End House at Stoke, and there the three sisters lived until their respective deaths. But Gray's dream of a life of lettered ease was at an end; he saw that what would support these ladies would leave but little margin for him. His temperament and his mode of study shut him out from every energetic profession. He was twenty-five years of age, and hitherto had not so much as begun any serious study of the law, for which his mother still imagined him to be preparing. Only one course was open to him, namely, to return to Cambridge, where living was very cheap, and to reside in college, spending his vacations quietly at Stoke Pogis. As Mason puts it, "he was too delicate to hurt two persons for whom he had so tender an affection, by peremptorily declaring his real intentions, and therefore changed, or pretended to change, the line of his study." Henceforward, until 1759, his whole life was a regular oscillation between Stoke and Cambridge, varied only by occasional visits to London. The first part of his life was now over. At twenty-five Gray becomes a middle-aged man, and loses, among the libraries of the University, his last pretensions to physical elasticity. From this time forward we find that his ailments, his melancholy, his reserve, and his habit of drowning consciousness in perpetual study, have taken firm hold upon him, and he begins to plunge into an excess of reading, treating the acquisition of knowledge as a narcotic. In the winter of 1742 he proceeded to Peterhouse, and taking his bachelor's degree in Civil Law, was forthwith installed as a resident of that college.

CHAPTER IV.

GRAY took up his abode at Peterhouse, in the room nearest the road on the second floor on the north side, a room which still exists and which commands a fine view of Pembroke College further east, on the opposite side of Trumpington Street. It would seem, indeed, that Gray's eyes and thoughts were for ever away from home, and paying a visit to the society across the road. His letters are full of minute discussions of what is going on at Pembroke, but never a word of Peterhouse ; indeed so naturally and commonly does he discuss the politics of the former college, often without naming it, that all his biographers, except of course Mason, seem to have taken for granted that he was describing Peterhouse. Oddly enough, Mason, who might have explained this circumstance in half a dozen words, does not appear to have noticed the fact, so natural did it seem to him to read about events which went on in his own college of Pembroke. Nor is it explained why Gray never became a fellow of Peterhouse. In all the correspondence of Gray I have only noted one solitary instance in which he has mentioned a Petrusian ; on this one occasion he does name the Master, J. Whalley, afterwards Bishop of Chester, in connexion with an anecdote which does more honour to him as a kind old

soul than as a disciplinarian.   But all Gray's friends, and
enemies, and interests, were centered in Pembroke, and
he shows such an intimate knowledge of all the cabals
and ridiculous little intrigues which thrilled the common-
room of that college, as requires an explanation that
now can never be given.   These first years of his residence are the most obscure in his whole career.   It must
be remembered that of his three most intimate correspondents one, West, was dead, another, Walpole, estranged,
and the third, Wharton, a resident in Cambridge like himself, and therefore too near at hand to be written to.   On
the 27th of December, 1742, a few days after his arrival
at the university, he wrote a letter to Dr. Wharton, which
has been preserved, and his *Hymn to Ignorance*, Mason
tells us, dates from the same time.   But after this he
entirely disappears from us for a couple of years, a few
legends of the direction taken by his studies and his
schemes of literary work being the only glimpses we get
of him.

   But although Gray tells us nothing about his own
college, it is still possible to form a tolerably distinct idea
of the society with whom he moved at Pembroke.   The
Master, Dr. Roger Long, was a man of parts, but full of
eccentricities, and gifted with a very disagreeable temper.
He was a species of poetaster, oddly associated in verse, at
different extremes of his long life, with Laurence Eusden,
the poet laureate, and the great Erasmus Darwin.   When
Gray settled in the University, Roger Long was sixty-two
years of age, had been Master of Pembroke nine years,
and, after being appointed Lowndes' Professor of astro-
nomy in 1750, was to survive until 1770, dying in his
ninety-first year.   He was fond of exercising his invention on lumbering constructions, which provoked the ridi-

cule of young wits like Gray; such as a sort of orrery
which he built in the north-eastern corner of the inner
court of Pembroke; and a still more remarkable water-
velocipede, upon which Dr. Long was wont to splash
about in Pembroke basin, "like a wild goose at play,"
heedless of mocking undergraduates. This eccentric personage was the object of much observation on the part of
Gray, who frequently mentioned him in his letters, and
was delighted when any new absurdity gave him an opportunity of writing to his correspondents about "the high
and mighty Prince Roger surnamed the Long, Lord of the
great Zodiac, the glass Uranium, and the Chariot that goes
without horses." As the astronomer grew older, he more
and more lost his authority with the fellows, and Gray
describes scenes of absolute rebellion which are, I believe,
recorded by no other historian. Gray was, undoubtedly,
in possession of information denied to the rest of the
world. Part of this information came, we cannot doubt,
from Dr. Wharton, and part from another intimate friend
of Gray's, William Trollope, who had taken his degree in
1730, and who was one of the senior fellows of Pembroke.
Another excellent friend of Gray's, also a leading man at
Pembroke, was the gentle and refined Dr. James Brown,
who eventually succeeded Long in the mastership, and in
whose arms Gray died. Outside this little Pembroke
circle Gray had few associates. He knew Conyers Middleton very well, and seems to have gained, a little later,
while haunting the rich library of Emmanuel College, the
acquaintance of a man whose influence on him was distinctly hurtful, the satellite of Warburton, Richard Hurd,
long afterwards Bishop of Worcester. But his association
with Conyers Middleton, certainly one of the most remarkable men then moving in the University, amounted almost

to friendship. They probably met nearly every day, Middleton being University Librarian; there was much that Gray would find sympathetic in the broad theology of Middleton, who had won his spurs by attacking the deists from ground almost as sceptical as their own, yet strictly within the pale of orthodoxy; nor would the irony and free thought of a champion of the Church of England be shocking to Gray, whose own tenets were at this time no less broad than his hatred of an open profession of deism was pronounced. Gray's feeling in religion seems to have been one of high and dry objection to enthusiasm, or change, or subversion. He was willing to admit a certain breadth of conjecture, so long as the forms of orthodoxy were preserved, but he objected excessively to any attempt to tamper with those forms, collecting Shaftesbury, Voltaire, Rousseau, and Hume under one general category of abhorrence. As he says in a cancelled stanza of one of his poems :—

> No more, with reason and thyself at strife,
> Give anxious cares and endless wishes room ;
> But through the cool sequester'd vale of life
> Pursue the silent tenour of thy doom,

an attitude which would not preclude a good deal of sympathy with the curious speculations of Conyers Middleton.

There is no doubt, however, that, in spite of a few companions of this class, most of them, like Middleton, much older than himself, he found Cambridge exceedingly dreary. He talks in one of his letters of "the strong attachment, or rather allegiance, which I and all here owe to our sovereign lady and mistress, the president of presidents, and head of heads (if I may be permitted to pronounce her name, that ineffable Octogrammaton), the

power of *Laziness.* You must know that she has been
pleased to appoint me (in preference to so many old servants of hers, who had spent their whole lives in quali-
fying themselves for the office) Grand Picker of Straws
and Push-Pin Player in ordinary to her Supinity." This
in 1744, and the same note had been struck two years
earlier in his curiously splenetic *Hymn to Ignorance :—*

> Hail, horrors, hail! ye ever gloomy bowers,
> Ye Gothic fanes, and antiquated towers,
> Where rushy Camus' slowly-winding flood
> Perpetual draws his humid train of mud :
> Glad I revisit thy neglected reign,
> O take me to thy peaceful shade again.

This atmosphere of apathy and ignorance was by no
means favourable to the composition of poetry. It was,
indeed absolutely fatal to it, and being at liberty to write
odes any hour of any day completely took away from the
poet the inclination to compose them at all. The flow of
verse which had been so full and constant in 1742 ceased
abruptly and entirely, and his thoughts turned in a wholly
fresh direction. He gave himself up almost exclusively
for the first four or five years to a consecutive study of
the whole existing literature of ancient Greece. If he
had seen cause to lament the deadness of classical enter-
prise at Cambridge when he was an undergraduate, this
lethargy had become still more universal since the death
of Bentley and Snape. Gray insisted, almost in solitude,
on the necessity of persistence in the cultivation of Greek
literature, and he forms the link between the school of
humanity which flourished in Cambridge in the beginning
of the eighteenth century, and that of which Porson was
to be the representative.

One of Gray's earliest schemes was a critical text

of Strabo, an author of whom he knew no satisfactory edition. Among the Pembroke MSS. may still be found his painstaking and copious notes collected for this purpose, and Mason possessed in Gray's handwriting " a great number of geographical disquisitions, particularly with respect to that part of Asia which comprehends Persia and India ; concerning the ancient and modern names and divisions of which extensive countries his notes are very copious." This edition of Strabo never came to the birth, and the same has to be said of his projected Plato, the notes for every section of which were in existence when Mason came to examine his papers. Another labour over which he toiled in vain was a text of the Greek Anthology, with translations of each separate epigram into Latin elegiac verse, a task on which he wasted months of valuable time, and which he then abandoned. His MS., however, of this last-mentioned work, came into his executors' hands, copied out as if for the press, with the addition, even, of a very full index, and it is a little surprising that Mason should not have hastened to oblige the world of classical students with a work which would have had a value at that time that it could not be said to possess now-a-days. Lord Chesterfield confidently " recommends the Greek epigrams to the supreme contempt " of his precious son, and in so doing gauged rightly enough the taste of the age. It would seem that Gray had the good sense to enjoy the delicious little poems of Meleager and his fellow-singers, but had not moral energy enough to insist on forcing them upon the attention of the world. He lamented, too, the neglect into which Aristotle had fallen, and determined to restore him to the notice of English scholars. As in the previous cases, however, his intentions remained unfulfilled, and

we turn with pleasure from the consideration of all this
melancholy waste of energy and learning. It is hard to
conceive of a sadder irony on the career of a scholar of
Gray's genius and accomplishment than is given by the
dismal contents of the so-called second volume of his
Works, published by Mathias in 1814, fragments and
jottings which bear the same relation to literature that
dough bears to bread.

The unfortunate difference with Horace Walpole came
to a close in the winter of 1744. A lady, probably Mrs.
Conyers Middleton, made peace between the friends.
Walpole expressed a desire that Gray would write to him,
and as Gray was passing through London on his way from
Cambridge to Stoke in the early part of November, a
meeting came off. The poet wrote Walpole a note as soon
as he arrived, " and immediately received a very civil answer." Horace Walpole was then living in the ministerial
neighbourhood of Arlington Street, and thither on the following evening Gray went to visit him. Gray's account to
Wharton of the interview is entertaining : "I was somewhat abashed at his confidence ; he came to meet me, kissed
me on both sides with all the ease of one who receives an
acquaintance just come out of the country, squatted me
into a fauteuil, began to talk of the town, and this and
that and t'other, and continued with little interruption
for three hours, when I took my leave very indifferently
pleased, but treated with monstrous good breeding. I
supped with him next night, as he desired. Ashton was
there, whose formalities tickled me inwardly, for he, I
found, was to be angry about the letter I had wrote him.
However, in going home together our hackney-coach
jumbled us up into a sort of reconciliation. . . . . Next
morning I breakfasted alone with Mr. Walpole ; when we

had all the éclaircissement I ever expected, and I left him much better satisfied than I had been hitherto." Gray's pride we see struggling against a very hearty desire in Walpole to let bygones be bygones ; the stately little poet, however, was not able to hold out against so many courteous seductions, and he gradually returned to his old intimacy and affection for Walpole. It is nevertheless doubtful whether he ever became so fond of the latter as Walpole was of him. He accepted the homage, however, to the end of his days, and was more admired perhaps, by Horace Walpole, and for a longer period, than any other person.

Perhaps in consequence of the " éclaircissement " with Walpole, Gray began at this time a correspondence with Mr. Chute and Mr. Whithead, the gentlemen with whom he had spent some months in Venice. Chute was a Hampshire squire, a dozen years senior to Gray and Walpole, but a great admirer of them both, and they both wrote to him some of their brightest letters. Chute was what our Elizabethan forefathers called " Italianate ;" he sympathized with Gray's tastes in music and statuary, vowed that life was not worth living north of the Alps, and spent the greater part of his time in Casa Ambrosio, Sir Horace Mann's house in Florence. He was an accomplished person, who played and sang, and turned a neat copy of verses, and altogether was a very agreeable exception among country gentlemen. He lived on until 1776, carefully preserving the letters he had interchanged with his sprightly friends.

About this time (May 30, 1744) Pope had died, and both Gray and Walpole refer frequently to the circumstance in their letters. It seems that Gray had had at least one interview with the great poet

of the age before him, an interview the date of
which it would be curious to ascertain. Gray's words
are interesting. He writes to Walpole (Feb. 3, 1746),
referring probably to the scandals about Atossa and the
Patriot King, "I can say no more for Mr. Pope, for what
you keep in reserve may be worse than all the rest. It
is natural to wish the finest writer,—one of them,—we
ever had, should be an honest man. It is for the interest
even of that virtue, whose friend he professed himself,
and whose beauties he sung, that he should not be found
a dirty animal. But, however, this is Mr. Warburton's
business, not mine, who may scribble his pen to the
stumps and all in vain, if these facts are so. *It is not
from what he told me about himself* that I thought well
of him, but from a humanity and goodness of heart, aye,
and greatness of mind, that runs through his private correspondence, not less apparent than are a thousand little
vanities and weaknesses mixed with those good qualities,
for nobody ever took him for a philosopher." There
exists a book in which Pope has written his own name,
and Gray his underneath, with a date in Pope's lifetime.
Evidently there had been personal intercourse between
them, in which Walpole may have had a part; for the
latter said, very late in his own career, " Remember, I
have lived with Gray and seen Pope."

In 1744 appeared two poems of some importance in
the history of eighteenth century literature, Akenside's
Pleasures of the Imagination and Armstrong's *Art of
Preserving Health*. Gray read them instantly, for the
authors were friends of his friend Wharton. The first
he found often obscure and even unintelligible, but yet in
many respects admirable ; and he checked himself in
the act of criticizing Akenside, " a very ingenious man,

worth fifty of myself." For Armstrong he showed less interest. The reading of these and other poems, a fresh beat of the pulse of English poetry in her fainting fit, set him thinking of his own neglected epic, the *De Principiis Cogitandi*, or "Master Tommy Lucretius" as he nicknamed it. This unwieldy production, however, could not be encouraged to flourish : " 'tis but a puleing chitt," says its author, and Mason tells us that about this time the posthumous publication of the *Anti-Lucretius* of the Cardinal Melchior de Polignac, a book long awaited and received at last with great disappointment, made Gray decide to let Locke and the Origin of Ideas alone. It may be noted that in July 1745 Gray had serious thoughts, which came to nothing, of moving over from Peterhouse to Trinity Hall.

We get glimpses of him now and then, from his letters. He does not entirely forget the pleasures of "strumming," he tells Chute ; "I look at my music now and then, that I may not forget it ;" and in September 1746 he has been writing "a few autumnal verses," the exact nature of which it is now impossible to specify. In August of the same year he had been in London, spending his mornings with Walpole in Arlington Street, and his afternoons at the trial of the Jacobite Lords. · His account of Kilmarnock and Cromartie is vivid, and not as unsympathetic as it might be. Now, as for many years to come, Gray usually went up to town in the middle of June, saw what was to be seen, proceeded to Stoke, and returned to Cambridge in September. Late in August 1746 Horace Walpole took a house within the precincts of the Castle of Windsor, and Gray at Stoke found this very convenient, for the friends were able to spend one day of each week together. In

May 1747 Walpole rented, and afterwards bought, that estate on the north bank of the Thames which he has made famous under the name of Strawberry Hill, and in future Gray scarcely ever passed a long vacation without spending some of his time there. It was now that his first poem was published. Walpole persuaded him to allow Dodsley to print the *Ode on a Distant Prospect of Eton College*, and it accordingly appeared anonymously, in the summer of 1747, as a thin folio pamphlet. In the autumn of this same year, while Gray was Walpole's guest at Strawberry Hill, he sat for the most pleasing, though the most feminine of his portraits, that by John Giles Eckhardt, a German who had come over with Vanloo, and to whom Walpole had addressed his poem of *The Beauties*. The *Eton Ode* fell perfectly stillborn, in spite of Walpole's enthusiasm; even less observed by the critics of the hour than Collins' little volume of *Odes*, which had appeared six months earlier. We may observe that Gray was now thirty years of age, and not only absolutely unknown, but not in the least persuaded in himself that he ought to be known.

It seems to have been about this time that the remarkable interview took place between Gray and Hogarth. The great painter, now in his fiftieth year, had just reached the summit of his reputation by completing his *Marriage à la Mode*, which Gray admired like the rest of the world. The vivacious Walpole thought that he would bring these interesting men together, and accordingly arranged a little dinner, from which he anticipated no small intellectual diversion. Unfortunately Hogarth was more surly and egotistical than usual, and Gray was plunged in one of his fits of melancholy reserve, so that Walpole had to rely entirely upon his own flow of spirits to prevent absolute silence, and vowed at the end of the repast that he had never been so dull in his life. To show, however, how Gray could sparkle when the cloud happened to rise from off his spirits, we may quote entire the delightful letter to Walpole, in which one of the brightest of his lesser poems first appeared :—

Cambridge, March 1, 1747.

As one ought to be particularly careful to avoid blunders in a compliment of condolence, it would be a sensible satisfaction to me, before I testify my sorrow, and the sincere part I take in your misfortune, to know for certain who it is I lament. I knew Zara and Selima (Selima, was it ? or Fatima ?), or rather I knew them both together; for I cannot justly say which was which. Then as to your "handsome Cat," the name you distinguish her by, I am no less at a loss, as well knowing one's handsome cat is always the cat one loves best; or if one be alive and one dead, it is usually the latter that is the handsomest. Besides, if the point were never so clear, I hope you do not think me so ill-bred or so imprudent as to forfeit all my interest in the survivor; oh, no! I would rather seem to mistake, and imagine to be sure it must be the tabby one that had met with this sad accident. Till this matter is a little better determined, you will excuse me if I do not begin to cry :—

"Tempus inane peto, requiem, spatiumque doloris."

Which interval is the more convenient, as it gives me time to rejoice with you on your new honours [Walpole had just been elected F.R.S.]. This is only a beginning; I reckon next week we shall hear you are a free-mason, or a Gormagon at least. Heigh ho! I feel (as you to be sure have long since) that I have very little to say, at least in prose. Somebody will be the better for it; I do not mean you, but your Cat, feue Mademoiselle Selime, whom I am about to immortalize for one week or fortnight, as follows :—

'Twas on a lofty vase's side
Where China's gayest art had dyed
    The azure flowers that blow,
The pensive Selima reclined,
Demurest of the tabby kind,
    Gaz'd on the lake below.

Her conscious tail her joy declar'd ;
The fair round face, the snowy beard,
    The velvet of her paws,
Her coat that with the tortoise vies,
Her ears of jet, and emerald eyes,
    She saw ; and purr'd applause.

Still had she gaz'd ; but midst the tide
Two beauteous forms were seen to glide,
    The Genii of the stream ;
Their scaly armour's Tyrian hue,
Through richest purple, to the view
    Betray'd a golden gleam.

The hapless Nymph with wonder saw :
A whisker first, and then a claw,
    With many an ardent wish,
She stretch'd, in vain, to reach the prize.
What female heart can gold despise ?
    What Cat's averse to fish ?

Presumptuous maid ! With looks intent
Again she stretched, again she bent,
    Nor knew the gulf between,
(Malignant Fate sat by, and smil'd.)
The slipp'ry verge her feet beguil'd,
    She tumbled headlong in.

Eight times emerging from the flood,
She mew'd to ev'ry wat'ry God ;
    Some speedy aid to send.
No Dolphin came, no Nereid stirr'd,
No cruel Tom nor Harry heard,
    What favourite has a friend ?

> From hence, ye beauties, undeceiv'd,
> Know one false step is ne'er retriev'd,
>   And be with caution bold.
> Not all that tempts your wand'ring eyes
> And heedless hearts is lawful prize,
>   Nor all, that glisters, gold.

There's a poem for you; it is rather too long for an Epitaph.

It is rather too long for a quotation, also, but the reader may find some entertainment in seeing so familiar a poem restored to its original readings. Johnson's comment on this piece is more unfortunate than usual. He calls it " a trifle, but not a happy trifle." Later critics have been unanimous in thinking it one of the happiest of all trifles; and there can be no doubt that in its ease and lightness it shows that Gray had been reading Gresset and Piron to advantage, and that he remembered the gay suppers with Mdlle. Quinault. A French poet of the neatest class, however, would certainly have avoided the specious little error detected by Johnson in the last line, and would not have laid himself open to the charge of supposing that what cats really like is not gold-fish, but gold itself.

We must return, however, to the dreary days in which Gray divided his leisure from Greek literature between drinking tar-water, on the recommendation of Berkeley's *Siris*, and observing the extraordinary quarrelling and bickering which went on in the combination-room at Pembroke. These dissensions reached a climax in the summer of 1746. The cause of the Master, Dr. Roger Long, was supported by a certain Dr. Andrews, while James Brown, popularly styled Obadiah Fusk, led the body of the fellows, with whom Gray sympathized. " Mr. Brown wants nothing but a foot in height and his

own hair to make him a little old Roman," we are told in
August of that year, and has been so determined that the
Master talks of calling in the Attorney-General to decide.
Even in the Long Vacation fellows of Pembroke can talk
of nothing else, and "tremble while they speak." Tuthill,
for some occult reason, is threatened with the loss of his
fellowship, and Gray at Stoke, in September 1746, will
hurry to Cambridge at any moment, so as not to be absent
during the Pembroke audit.

All this time not one word is said of his own
college. Nor was he always so anxious to return to
Cambridge. In the winter of 1746 he had a very
bright spell of enjoyment in London. "I have been
in town," he says to Wharton (Dec. 11th), "flaunt-
ing about at public places of all kinds with my two
Italianized friends [Chute and Whithead]. The world
itself has some attractions in it to a solitary of six
years' standing; and agreeable, well-meaning people of
sense (thank Heaven there are so few of them) are my
peculiar magnet; it is no wonder, then, if I felt some
reluctance at parting with them so soon, or if my spirits,
when I return to my cell, should sink for a time, not
indeed to storm or tempest, but a good deal below change-
able." He was considerably troubled by want of money
at this time ; he had been to town partly to sell off a little
stock, to pay an old debt, and had found the rate of
exchange so low that he would have lost twelve per cent.
He was saved from this necessity by a timely loan from
Wharton. He spent his leisure at Christmas in making
a great chronological table, the form of which long afterwards suggested to Henry Clinton his *Fasti Hellenici*.
Gray's work began with the 30th Olympiad, and was
brought down to the 113th, covering therefore 332

years. Each page of it was divided into nine columns, one for the Olympiad, the second for the Archons, the third for the public affairs of Greece, the fourth, fifth and sixth for the Philosophers, the seventh for the Poets, the eighth for the Historians, and the ninth for the Orators.

The same letter which announces this performance mentions the *Odes* of Collins and Joseph Warton. Gray had been briskly supplied with these little books, which had only been published a few days before. The former was the important volume, but the public bought the latter. Gray's comment on Warton and Collins is remarkable : "Each is the half of a considerable man, and one the counterpart of the other. The first has but little invention, very poetical choice of expression, and a good ear. The second, a fine fancy, modelled upon the antique, a bad ear, great variety of words and images, with no choice at all. They both deserve to last some years, *but will not.*" This last clause is an example of the vanity of prophesying. It is difficult to understand what Gray meant by accusing Collins of a "bad ear," the one thing in which Collins was undoubtedly Gray's superior ; in other respects the criticism, though unsympathetic, is not without acumen, and for bad or good, was the most favourable thing said of Collins for many years to come. In 1748 Gray and Collins were destined to meet, for once during their lives, between the covers of the same book, at which we shall presently arrive.

Gray was thirty years old on the day that he read Collins' *Odes*. He describes himself as " lazy and listless and old and vexed and perplexed," with all human evils but the gout, which was soon to follow. The proceedings at Pembroke had reached such a pass that Gray

began to sympathize with the poor old Master, him of the
water-velocipede. The fellows had now grown so rebellious as to abuse him roundly to his face, never to go
into combination-room till he went out, or if he entered
while they were there to continue sitting even in his own
magisterial chair. They would bicker with him about
twenty paltry matters, till he would lose his temper, and
tell them they were impertinent. Gray turned from all
this to a scheme which he had long had in view, the
publication of his friend West's poems. Walpole proposed that he should bring out these and his own odes
in a single volume, and Gray was not disinclined to carry
out this notion. But when he came to put their "joint-
stock" together, he found it insufficient in bulk. Nor,
as we have already seen, did the few and scattered verses
of West see the light till long after the death of Gray.
All that came of this talk of printing, was the anonymous
publication of the *Eton Ode*. Meanwhile, as he says to
Wharton, in March 1747, "my works are not so considerable as you imagine. I have read Pausanias and
Athenæus all through, and Æschylus again. I am now
in Pindar and Lysias, for I take Verse and Prose together
like bread and cheese."

About this time the excellent Wharton married and
left Cambridge. A still worse misfortune happened
to Gray in the destruction of his house in Cornhill,
which was burned down in May 1748. He seems
to have been waked up a little by this disaster, and to
have spent seven weeks in town as the guest of various
friends, who were "all so sorry for my loss that I
could not choose but laugh : one offered me opera tickets,
insisted upon carrying me to the grand masquerade,
desired me to sit for my picture ; others asked me to

their concerts, or dinners and suppers at their houses; or hoped I would drink chocolate with them while I stayed in town. All my gratitude,— or, if you please, my revenge,—was to accept everything they offered me; if it had been but a shilling I should have taken it : thank Heaven, I was in good spirits, else I could not have done it." London was amusing for him at this time, with Horace Walpole flying between Arlington Street and Strawberry Hill, and Chute and his nephew Whithead full of sprightly gaieties and always glad to see him. Whithead, who was in the law, undertook with success about this time some legal business for Gray, the exact nature of which does not appear, and the poet describes him as " a fine young personage in a coat all over spangles, just come over from the tour of Europe to take possession and be married. Say I wish him more spangles, and more estates, and more wives." Poor Whithead did not live long enough to marry one wife; while his engagement loitered on he fell ill of a galloping consumption, and died in 1751, his death being accelerated by the imprudence of his brother, a clergyman, who insisted on taking him out hunting when he ought to have been in bed. Gray's house in Cornhill had been insured for 500*l.*, but the expenses of rebuilding it amounted to 650*l.* One of his aunts, probably Miss Antrobus, made him a present of 100*l.*; another aunt, still more probably Mrs. Oliffe, lent him an equal sum for his immediate wants on a decent rate of interest, and for the remainder he was indebted to the kindness of Wharton. It appears from all this that Gray's income was strictly bounded, at that time, to his actual expenses, and that he had no margin whatever. He declined, in fact, in June 1748, an invitation from Dr. Wharton to come and stay with him in the

north of England, on the ground that "the good people here
[at Stoke] would think me the most careless and ruinous
of mortals, if I should think of a journey at this time."

In the letter from which a quotation has just been
given, Gray mentions for the first time a man whose
name was to be inseparably associated with his own,
without whose pious care for his memory, indeed, the
task of writing Gray's life in any detail would be impossible. In the year 1747 Gray's attention was directed
by a friend to a modest publication of verses in imitation
of Milton; the death of Pope was sung in an elegy called
Musœus, to resemble *Lycidas*, and Milton's odes found
counterparts in *Il Bellicoso* and *Il Pacifico*. These pieces,
which were not entirely without a meritorious ease of
metre, were the production of William Mason, a young
man of twenty-two, the son of a Yorkshire clergyman,
and a scholar of St. John's College, Cambridge. His intelligence first attracted the notice of a fellow of his own
college, Dr. William Heberden, the distinguished Professor of Medicine, who was a friend of Gray, and who
was very possibly the person who showed Mason's poems
to the latter. In the course of the same year, 1747,
through the exertions of Heberden and Gray, Mason was
nominated a fellow of Pembroke, and proposed to himself
to enter that remarkable bear-garden. But Dr. Roger
Long refused his consent, and it was not until February
1749, and after much litigation, that Mason was finally
elected.

There was something about Mason which Gray liked,
a hearty simplicity and honest ardour that covered a
good deal of push which Gray thought vulgar and did
not hesitate to chastise. Mason, on his side, was a faithful and affectionate henchman, full of undisguised admira-

tion of Gray and fear of his sarcasm, not unlike Boswell
in his persistence, and in his patience in enduring the
reproofs of the great man. Gray constantly crushed
Mason, but the latter was never offended, and after a
few tears, returned manfully to the charge. Gray's description of him in the second year of their acquaintance,
when Mason was only twenty-three, was this :—" Mason
has much fancy, little judgment, and a good deal of
modesty. I take him for a good and well-meaning creature ; but then he is really in simplicity a child, and
loves everybody he meets with ; he reads little or nothing,
writes abundance, and that with a desire to make
his fortune by it." This literary fluency was a matter of
wonder to Gray, whose own attar of roses was distilled
slowly and painfully, drop by drop, and all through life
he was apt to overrate Mason's verses. It was very difficult, of course, for him to feel unfavourably towards a
friend so enthusiastic and so anxious to please, and we
cannot take Gray's earnest approval of Mason's odes and
tragedies too critically. Moreover, he was Gray's earliest
and most slavish disciple ; before he left St. John's to
come within the greater poet's more habitual influence,
he had begun to imitate poems which he can only have
seen in manuscript.

Henceforward, in spite of his somewhat coarse and
superficial nature, in spite of his want of depth in
imagination and soundness in scholarship, in spite
of a general want of the highest qualities of character,
Mason became a great support and comfort to Gray.
His physical vigour and versatility, his eagerness in the
pursuit of literature, his unselfish ardour and loyalty,
were refreshing to the more fastidious and retiring man,
who enjoyed, moreover, the chance of having at last

found a person with whom he could discourse freely
about literature, in that constant easy interchange of impressions which is the luxury of a purely literary life.
Moreover, we must do Mason the justice to say that he
supplied to Gray's fancy whatever stimulus such a mind
as his was calculated to offer, receiving his smallest and
most fragmentary effusions with interest, encouraging him
to the completion of his poems, and receiving each fresh
ode as if a new planet had risen above the horizon. With
Walpole to be playful with, and Mason to be serious
with, Gray was no longer for the rest of his life exposed
to that east wind of solitary wretchedness which had
parched him for the first three years of his life at Cambridge.   At the same time, grateful as we must be to
Mason for his affection and goodheartedness, we cannot
refrain from wishing that his poems had been fastened
to a millstone and cast into the river Cam.   They are
not only barren and pompous to the very last degree,
but to the lovers of Gray they have this disadvantage
that they constantly resolve that poet's true sublime
into the ridiculous, and leave on the ear an uncomfortable echo, as of a too successful burlesque or parody.
Of this Gray himself was not unconscious, though he
put the thought behind him, as one inconsistent with
friendship.

A disreputable personage who crossed Gray's orbit about
this time, and was the object of his cordial dislike and
contempt, has left on the mind of posterity a sense of
higher natural gifts than any possessed by the respectable
Mason.   Christopher Smart, long afterwards author of
the *Song to David*, was an idle young man who had
been admitted to Pembroke in October 1739, under
the protection of the Earl of Darlington, and who in

1745 was elected a fellow of his college. As early as
1740 he began to be celebrated for the wit and originality
of his Latin tripos verses, of which a series are still in
existence. One of these, a droll celebration of the
Nativity of Yawning, is not unlike Gray's own *Hymn to
Ignorance* in its contempt for the genius of Cambridge.
But Smart lost credit by his pranks and levities no less
quickly than he gained it by his skill. Gray writes in
March 1747 that Smart's debts are increasing daily, and
that he drinks hartshorn from morning till night. A
month later he had scandalized the university by per-
forming in the Zodiac Room, a club which had been
founded in 1725, a play of his own called a *A Trip to
Cambridge, or the Grateful Fair*, a piece which was never
printed and now no longer is in existence. Already, at this
time, Gray thought Smart mad. " He can't hear his own
Prologue without being ready to die with laughter. He
acts five parts himself, and is only sorry he can't do all
the rest. . . . . As for his vanity and faculty of lying,
they have come to their full maturity. All this, you see,
must come to a jail, or Bedlam." It did come to Bedlam,
in 1763, but not until Smart had exhausted every eccen-
tricity and painful folly possible to man. But the minor
catastrophe was much nearer, namely the jail. In
November 1747 he was arrested at the suit of a London
tailor, was got out of prison by means of a subscription
made in the college, and received a sound warning to
behave better in future, a warning which Gray, who
watched him narrowly and noted his moral symptoms
with cold severity, justly predicted would be entirely
frustrated by his drunkenness.

The frequent disturbances caused in the university by
such people as Smart had by this time led to much public

scandal. Gray says "the fellow commoners—the bucks
—are run mad, they set women upon their heads in the
streets at noon-day, break open shops, game in the coffee-
houses on Sundays, and in short," he adds in angry irony,
"act after my own heart." The Tuns Tavern at Cambridge
was the scene of nightly orgies, in which professors and
fellows set an example of roistering to the youth of the
University. Heavy bills were run up at inns and coffee-
houses, which were afterwards repudiated with effrontery.
The breaking of windows and riots in public parts of the
town were indulged in to such an extent as to make
Cambridge almost intolerable, and the work of James
Brown, Gray's intimate friend, who held the post of Senior
Proctor, was far from being a sinecure. In 1748, the
Duke of Somerset, who had absolutely neglected his re-
sponsibilities, was succeeded in the Chancellorship by the
Duke of Newcastle, whose installation promised little
hope of reform. Gray described the scene to Wharton :—
"Every one while it lasted was very gay and very busy
in the morning, and very owlish and very tipsy at night :
I make no exception from the Chancellor to blue-coat,"
who was the vice-chancellor's servant. However, it presently appeared that the Duke of Newcastle was not
inclined to sacrifice discipline. The Bishops united with
him in concocting a plan by which the licence of the
resident members of the university should be checked,
and in May 1750 the famous code of *Orders and Regu-
lations* was brought before the Senate. It was not, however, easy to restore order to a community which had so
long been devoted to the Lord of Misrule, and it was not
until more than twenty persons of good family had been
"expelled or rusticated for very heinous violations of our
laws and discipline" that anything like decent behaviour
was restored, the fury of the undergraduates displaying

itself in a final outburst of mutiny, in which they rushed along the streets brandishing lighted links.

This scene of rebellion and confusion could not fail to excite strong emotion in the mind of a man like Gray, of orderly tastes and timid personal character, to whom a painted Indian would be scarcely a more formidable object that a noisy young buck, flushed with wine, flinging his ash-stick against college windows, and his torch into the faces of passers-by. A life at the university given up to dice, and horses, and the loud coarse Georgian dissipation of that day, could not seem to a thinker to be one which brought glory either to the teacher or the taught, and in the midst of this sensual riot Gray sat down to write his poem on *The Alliance of Education and Government.* Of his philosophical fragments this is by far the best, and it is seriously to be regretted that it does not extend beyond one hundred and ten lines. The design of the poem, which has been preserved, is highly interesting, and the treatment at least as poetical as that of so purely didactic a theme could be. Short as it is, it attracted the warm enthusiasm of Gibbon, who ejaculates :—"instead of compiling tables of chronology and natural history, why did not Mr. Gray apply the powers of his genius to finish the philosophical poem of which he has left such an exquisite specimen ?" The heroic couplet is used with great skill ; as an example may be cited the lines describing the invasion of Italy by the Goths :—

> As oft have issued, host impelling host,
> The blue-eyed myriads from the Baltic coast ;
> The prostrate South to the destroyer yields
> Her boasted titles and her golden fields :
> With grim delight the brood of winter view
> A brighter day, and heavens of azure hue,
> Scent the new fragrance of the breathing rose,
> And quaff the pendant vintage as it grows.

while one line, at least, lives in the memory of every lover of poetry :—

> When love could teach a monarch to be wise,
> *And gospel-light first dawn'd from Bullen's eyes.*

On the 19th of August, 1748, Gray copied the first fifty-seven lines of this poem in a letter he was writing to Wharton, saying that his object would be to show that education and government must concur in order to produce great and useful men. But as he was pursuing his plan in the leisurely manner habitual to him, Montesquieu's celebrated work *L'Esprit des Lois* was published, and fell into his hands. He found, as he told Mason, that the Baron had forestalled some of his best thoughts, and from this time forth his interest in the scheme languished and soon after it entirely lapsed. Some years later he thought of taking it up again, and was about to compose a prefatory *Ode to M. de Montesquieu* when that writer died, on the 10th of February, 1755, and the whole thing was abandoned. Gray's remarks on *L'Esprit des Lois* are in his clearest and acutest vein :—" The subject is as extensive as mankind ; the thoughts perfectly new, generally admirable, as they are just ; sometimes a little too refined ; in short there are faults, but such as an ordinary man could never have committed : the style very lively and concise, consequently sometimes obscure,—it is the gravity of Tacitus, whom he admires, tempered with the gaiety and fire of a Frenchman." Gray was probably the only Englishman living capable of criticising a new French book with this delicate justice.

CHAPTER V.

EARLY in 1748 Dodsley published the first three volumes
of his useful miscellany, called *A Collection of Poems*,
for the plan of which he claimed an originality that it
scarcely deserved, since, like the earlier miscellanies of
Gildon and Tonson, it merely aimed at embracing in one
work the best scattered poetry of the day.   In the second
volume were printed, without the author's name, three of
Gray's odes—those *To Spring*, *On Mr. Walpole's Cat*, and
the *Eton Ode*.   Almost all the poets of this age, and
several of the preceding, were contributors to the collection.   Pope, Green, and Tickell represented the past
generation, while Collins, Dyer, and Shenstone, in the
first volume ; Lyttelton, Gilbert West, I. H. Browne, and
Edwards the sonneteer, in the second volume ; and Joseph
Warton, Garrick, Mason, and Walpole himself in the
third volume, showed to the best of their ability what
English poetry in that age was capable of ; while three
sturdy Graces, bare and bold, adorned the title-page of
each instalment, and gave a kind of visible pledge that
no excess of refinement should mar the singing, even
when Lowth, Bishop of London, held the lyre.

As in the crisis of a national history some young man,

unknown before, leaps to the front by sheer force of
character, and takes the helm of state before his elders,
so in the confusion and mutiny at the University the
talents of Dr. Edmund Keene, the new master of Peterhouse, came suddenly into notice, and from comparative
obscurity he rose at once into the fierce light that beats
upon a successful reformer. His energy and promptitude
pointed him out as a fit man to become vice-chancellor in
the troublous year 1749, although he was only thirty-six
years of age, and it was practically owing to his quick
eye and hard hand that order was reinstated in the
university. With his mastership of the college Gray
began to take an interest for the first time in Peterhouse,
and cultivated the acquaintance of Keene, in whom he
discovered an energy and practical power which he had
never suspected. The reign of Mum Sharp, as the undergraduates nicknamed Keene, was as brief as it was
brilliant. In 1752 the Government rewarded his action
in the university with the see of Chester, and two years
later he resigned his nominal headship of Peterhouse,
dying Bishop of Ely nearly thirty years afterwards.

At Pembroke Hall, meanwhile, all was going well at last.
In the spring of 1749 there was a pacification between
the Master and the Fellows, and Pembroke, says Gray to
Wharton, "is all harmonious and delightful." But the
rumours of dissension had thinned the ranks of the
undergraduates; "they have no boys at all, and unless
you can send us a hamper or two out of the north to begin
with, they will be like a few rats straggling about a
deserted dwelling-house."

Gray was now about to enter the second main period of
his literary activity, and he opens it with a hopeless pro-
testation of his apathy and idleness. He writes (April

25, 1749), from Cambridge, this amusing piece of pro-
phecy : — " The spirit of laziness, the spirit of this place,
begins to possess even me, that have so long declaimed
against it. Yet has it not so prevailed, but that I feel
that discontent with myself, that *ennui* that ever accom-
panies it in its beginnings. Time will settle my con-
science, time will reconcile my languid companion ; we
shall smoke, we shall tipple, we shall doze together, we
shall have our little jokes, like other people, and our long
stories. Brandy will finish what port began ; and a
month after the time you will see in some corner of a
London Evening Post, yesterday, died the Rev. Mr. John
Grey, Senior Fellow of Clare Hall, a facetious companion,
and well respected by all that knew him. His death is
supposed to have been occasioned by a fit of the apoplexy,
being found fallen out of bed." But this whimsical anti-
cipation of death and a blundering mortuary inscription,
was startled out of his thoughts by the sudden approach
of death itself to one whom he dearly loved. His aunt,
Miss Mary Antrobus, died somewhat suddenly, at the age
of sixty-six, at Stoke, on the 5th of November, 1749.
The letter which Gray wrote to his mother on receiving
news of this event is so characteristic of his wise and
tender seriousness of character, and allows us to observe so
much more closely than usual the real working of his
mind, that no apology is needed for quoting it here. It
was written from Cambridge, on the 7th of November,
1749 :—

The unhappy news I have just received from you equally
surprises and afflicts me. I have lost a person I loved very
much, and have been used to from my infancy ; but am much
more concerned for your loss, the circumstances of which I for-
bear to dwell upon, as you must be too sensible of them yourself ;

and will, I fear, more and more need a consolation that no one
can give, except He who had preserved her to you so many
years, and at last, when it was His pleasure, has taken her from
us to Himself; and perhaps, if we reflect upon what she felt in
this life, we may look upon this as an instance of His goodness
both to her and to those that loved her. She might have languished many years before our eyes in a continual increase of
pain, and totally helpless; she might have long wished to end
her misery without being able to attain it; or perhaps even lost
all sense and yet continued to breathe; a sad spectacle for such
as must have felt more for her than she could have done for
herself. However you may deplore your own loss, yet think that
she is at last easy and happy : and has now more occasion to
pity us than we her. I hope, and beg, you will support yourself
with that resignation we owe to Him, who gave us our being for
good, and who deprives us of it for the same reason. I would
have come to you directly, but you do not say whether you
desire I should or not; if you do, I beg I may know it, for
there is nothing to hinder me, and I am in very good health.

It is impossible to imagine anything more sweet-
natured and unaffected than this letter, and it opens to us
for a moment the closed and sacred book of Gray's home-
life, those quiet autumn days of every year so peacefully
spent in loving and being loved by these three placid old
ladies at Stoke, in a warm atmosphere of musk and pot-
pourri.

The death of his aunt seems to have brought to his
recollection the *Elegy in a Country Churchyard*, begun
seven years before within sight of the ivy-clustered spire
under whose shadow she was laid. He seems to have
taken it in hand again, at Cambridge, in the winter of
1749, and tradition, which would fain see the poet always
writing in the very precincts of a churchyard, has fabled
that he wrote some stanzas among the tombs of Gran-

chester. He finished it, however, as he began it, at
Stoke Pogis, giving the last touches to it on the 12th of
June, 1750. "Having put an end to a thing whose
beginning you have seen long ago," he writes on that day
to Horace Walpole, "I immediately send it to you. You
will, I hope, look upon it in the light of a thing with an
end to it : a merit that most of my writings have wanted,
and are like to want." Walpole was only too highly
delighted with this latest effusion of his friend, in which
he was acute enough to discern the elements of a lasting
success. It is curious to reflect upon the modest and
careless mode in which that poem was first circulated
which was destined to enjoy and to retain a higher reputation in literature than any other English poem, perhaps
than any other poem of the world, written between
Milton and Wordsworth. The fame of the *Elegy* has
spread to all countries, and has exercised an influence on
all the poetry of Europe, from Denmark to Italy, from
France to Russia. With the exception of certain works
of Byron and Shakespeare, no English poem has been so
widely admired and imitated abroad ; and after more than
a century of existence, we find it as fresh as ever, when
its copies, even the most popular of all, those of Lamar-
tine, are faded and tarnished. It possesses the charm of
incomparable felicity, of a melody that is not too subtle
to charm every ear, of a moral persuasiveness that appeals
to every generation, and of metrical skill that in each
line proclaims the master. The *Elegy* may almost be
looked upon as the typical piece of English verse, our
poem of poems ; not that it is the most brilliant or
original or profound lyric in our language, but because it
combines in more balanced perfection than any other all
the qualities that go to the production of a fine poetical

H

effect. The successive criticisms of a swarm of Dryas-
dusts, each depositing his drop of siccative, the boundless
vogue and consequent profanation of stanza upon stanza,
the changes of fashion, the familiarity that breeds indifference, all these things have not succeeded in destroy-
ing the vitality of this humane and stately poem. The
solitary writer of authority who since the death of
Johnson has ventured to depreciate Gray's poetry, Mr.
Swinburne, who, in his ardour to do justice to Collins,
has been deeply and extravagantly unjust to the greater
man, even he, coming to curse, has been obliged to bless
this "poem of such high perfection and such universal
appeal to the tenderest and noblest depths of human
feeling," admitting, again, with that frankness which
makes Mr. Swinburne the most generous of disputants,
that "as an elegiac poet, Gray holds for all ages to come
his unassailable and sovereign station."

We may well leave to its fate a poem with so splendid
a history, a poem more thickly studded with phrases that
have become a part and parcel of colloquial speech than
any other piece, even of Shakespeare's, consisting of so few
consecutive lines. A word or two however may not be out
of place in regard to its form and the literary history of its
composition. The heroic quatrain, in the use of which
here and elsewhere, Gray easily excels all other English
writers, was not new to our literature. Among the Pembroke MSS. I find copious notes by Gray on the *Nosce
Teipsum* of Sir John Davies, a beautiful philosophical
poem first printed in 1599, and composed in this measure.
Davenant had chosen the same for his fragmentary epic
of *Gondibert*, and Dryden for his metallic and gorgeous
poem of the *Annus Mirabilis*. All these essays were certainly known to Gray, and he was possibly not uninfluenced

by the *Love Elegies* of James Hammond, a young cousin
of Horace Walpole's, who had died in 1742, and had
affected to be the Tibullus of the age.   Hammond had
more taste than genius, yet after reading, with much
fatigue, his forgotten elegies, I cannot avoid the impression
that Gray was influenced by this poetaster, in the matter
of form, more than by any other of his contemporaries.   A
familiar quatrain of West :—

> Ah me ! what boots us all our boasted power,
> Our golden treasure and our purple state !
> They cannot ward the inevitable hour,
> Nor stay the fearful violence of fate,

was probably the wild-wood stock on which Gray grafted
his wonderful rose of roses, borrowing something from all
his predecessors, but justifying every act of plagiarism by
the brilliance of his new combination.   Even the tiresome
sing-song of Hammond became in Gray's hands an instrument of infinite variety and beauty, as if a craftsman by
the mere touch of his fingers should turn ochre into gold.
The measure, itself, from first to last, is an attempt to
render in English the solemn alternation of passion and
reserve, the interchange of imploring and desponding tones,
that is found in the Latin elegiac, and Gray gave his
poem, when he first published it, an outward resemblance
to the text of Tibullus by printing it without any stanzaic
pauses.   It is in this form and with the original spelling
that the poem appears in an exquisite little volume, privately printed a few years ago at the Cambridge University
Press, in which Mr. Munro has placed his own Ovidian
translation of the *Elegy* opposite the original text ; as
pretty a tribute as was ever paid by one great University
scholar to the memory of another.

Walpole's enthusiasm for the *Elegy in a Country Church-yard* led him to commit the grave indiscretion of handing it about from friend to friend, and even of distributing manuscript copies of it, without Gray's cognizance. At the Manor House at Stoke Lady Cobham, who seems to have known Horace Walpole, read the *Elegy in a Country Churchyard* in manuscript before it had been many months in existence, and conceived a violent desire to know the author. So quiet was Gray, and so little inclined to assert his own personality, that she was unaware that he and she had lived together in the same country parish for several years, until a Rev. Mr. Robert Purt, a Cambridge fellow settled at Stoke, told her that, "thereabouts there lurked a wicked imp they call a poet." Mr. Purt, how-ever, enjoyed a very slight acquaintance with Gray (he was offended shortly afterwards at the introduction of his name into the *Long Story*, and very properly died of small-pox immediately), and could not venture to introduce him to her ladyship. Lady Cobham, however, had a guest staying with her, a Lady Schaub, who knew a friend of Gray's, a Lady Brown. On this very meagre introduction, Lady Schaub and Miss Speed, the niece of Lady Cobham, were persuaded by her ladyship, who shot her arrow like Teucer from behind the shield of Ajax, to call boldly upon Gray. They did so in the summer of 1751, but when they had crossed the fields to West End House, they found that the poet had gone out for a walk. They begged the ladies to say nothing of their visit, but they left among the papers in Gray's study this piquant little note : "Lady Schaub's compliments to Mr. Gray ; she is sorry not to have found him at home, to tell him that Lady Brown is very well." This little adventure assumed the hues of mystery and romance in so uneventful life as Gray's, and curiosity combined with good manners to make him put his shyness in his pocket and return Lady Schaub's polite but eccentric call. That far-reaching spider, the Viscountess Cobham, had now fairly caught him in her web, and for the remaining nine years of her life, she and her niece Miss Speed were his fast friends. Indeed his whole life might have been altered if Lady Cobham had had her way, for it seems certain that she would have been highly pleased to have seen him the husband of Harriet Speed and inheritor of the fortunes of the family. At one time Gray seems to have been really frightened lest they should marry him suddenly, against his will ; and perhaps he almost wished they would. At all events the only lines of his which can be called amatory were addressed to Miss Speed. She was seven years his junior, and when she was nearly forty she married a very young French officer, and went to live abroad, to which events, not uninteresting to Gray, we shall return in their proper place.

The romantic incidents of the call just described inspired Gray with his fantastic account of them given in the *Long Story*. He dwells on the ancient seat of the Huntingdons and Hattons, from the door of which one morning issued

> A brace of warriors, not in buff,
>   But rustling in their silks and tissues.
>
> The first came cap-a-pee from France,
>   Her conquering destiny fulfilling,
> Whom meaner beauties eye askance,
>   And vainly ape her art of killing.
>
> The other amazon kind heaven
>   Had armed with spirit, wit and satire ;
> But Cobham had the polish given,
>   And tipped her arrows with good-nature.

> With bonnet blue and capuchine,
>   And aprons long, they hid their armour;
> And veiled their weapons, bright and keen,
>   In pity to the country farmer.

These warriors sallied forth in the cause of a lady of high degree, who had just heard that the parish contained a poet, and who

> Swore by her coronet and ermine,
>   She'd issue out her high commission
> To rid the manor of such vermin.

At last they discover his lowly haunt, and bounce in without so much as a tap at the door.

> The trembling family they daunt,
>   They flirt, they sing, they laugh, they tattle,
> Rummage his mother, pinch his aunt,
>   And upstairs in a whirlwind rattle:
>
> Each hole and cupboard they explore,
>   Each creek and cranny of his chamber,
> Run hurry-scurry round the floor,
>   And o'er the bed and tester clamber:
>
> Into the drawers and china pry,
>   Papers and books, a huge imbroglio,
> Under a tea-cup he might lie,
>   Or creased, like dog's-ears, in a folio.

The pitying Muses, however, have conveyed him away, and the proud amazons are obliged to retreat; but they have the malignity to leave a spell behind them, which their victim finds when he slinks back to his home.

> The words too eager to unriddle
>   The poet felt a strange disorder;
> Transparent bird-lime formed the middle,
>   And chains invisible the border.

> So cunning was the apparatus,
>   The powerful pot-hooks did so move him,
> That will he, nill he, to the great house
>   He went as if the devil drove him.

When he arrives at the Manor House, of course, he is dragged before the great lady, and is only saved from destruction by her sudden fit of clemency :—

> The ghostly prudes with haggard face
>   Already had condemned the sinner.
> My lady rose, and with a grace—
>   She smiled, and bid him come to dinner.

All this is excellent fooling, charmingly arch and easy in its humorous romance, and highly interesting as a picture of Gray's home-life. In the Pembroke MS. of the *Long Story*, he says that he wrote it in August 1750. It was included in the semi-private issue of the *Six Poems* in 1753, but in no other collection published during Gray's life-time. He considered its allusions too personal to be given to the public.

In this one instance Walpole's indiscretion in circulating the *Elegy* brought Gray satisfaction ; in others it annoyed him. On the 10th of February, 1751, he received a rather impertinently civil letter from the publisher of a periodical called the *Magazine of Magazines*, coolly informing him that he was actually printing his " ingenious poem called reflections in a Country Church-yard," and praying for his indulgence and the honour of his correspondence. Gray immediately wrote to Horace Walpole (Feb. 11th) :—" As I am not at all disposed to be either so indulgent or so correspondent as they desire, I have but one bad way left to escape the honour they would inflict upon me : and therefore am obliged to desire

you would make Dodsley print it immediately (which
may be done in less than a week's time) from your copy,
but without my name, in what form is most convenient
for him, but on his best paper and character; he must
correct the press himself, and print it without any
interval between the stanzas, because the sense is in some
places continued without them." All this was done with
extraordinary promptitude, and five days after this letter
of Gray's, on the 16th of February, 1751, Dodsley published a large quarto pamphlet, anonymous, price sixpence,
entitled *An Elegy wrote in a Country Church-Yard*. It
was preceded by a short advertisement, unsigned, but
written by Horace Walpole. At this point may be in-
serted a note, which Gray has appended in the margin
of the Pembroke MS. of this poem. It settles a point of
bibliography which has been discussed by commentator
after commentator :—

Published in Feb^ry, 1751, by Dodsley, & went thro' four
editions, in two months; and afterwards a fifth, 6th, 7th, &
8th, 9th, 10th, & 11th, printed also in 1753 with Mr. Bentley's
Designs, of wch there is a 2^d edition, & again by Dodsley in
his Miscellany vol. 4th & in a Scotch Collection call'd the
Union ; translated into Latin by Chr: Anstey, Esq. and the Rev^d
Mr Roberts, & published in 1762, & again in the same year by
Rob: Lloyd, M.A.

Gray here cites fifteen authorized editions of the English
text of the *Elegy ;* its pirated editions were countless.
The *Magazine of Magazines* persisted, although Gray had
been neither indulgent nor correspondent, and the poem
appeared in the issue for February, published, as was then
the habit of periodicals, on the last of that month. The
London Magazine stole it for its issue for March, and the
Grand Magazine of Magazines copied it in April. Every-

body read it, in town and country ; Shenstone, far away
from the world of books, had seen it before the 28th of
March. It achieved a complete popular success from the
very first, and the name of its author gradually crept into
notoriety. The attribution of the *Elegy* to Gray was
more general than has been supposed. A pamphlet,
printed soon after this date, speaks of " the Maker of the
Churchyard Essay " as being a Cambridge celebrity whose
claims to preferment had been notoriously overlooked ;
and by far the cleverest of all the parodies, *An Evening
Contemplation*, 1753, a poem of special interest to
students of university manners, is preceded by an
elaborate compliment to Gray. The success of his poem,
however, brought him little direct satisfaction, and no
money. He gave the right of publication to Dodsley, as he
did in all other instances. He had a Quixotic notion
that it was beneath a gentleman to take money for his
inventions from a bookseller, a view in which Dodsley
warmly coincided ; and it was stated by an another bookseller, who after Gray's death contended with Mason,
that Dodsley was known to have made nearly a thousand
pounds by the poetry of Gray. Mason had no such
scruples as his friend, and made frantic efforts to regain
Gray's copyright, launching vainly into litigation on the
subject, and into unseemly controversy.

The autumn of 1750 had been marked in Gray's
uneventful annals by the death of Dr. Middleton, and by
the visit of a troublesome Indian cousin, Mrs. Forster,
who stayed a month in London, and wearied Gray by her
insatiable craving after sight-seeing. In Conyers Middleton, who died on the 28th of July, 1750, at the age of
sixty-seven, Gray lost one of his most familiar and most
intellectual associates, a person of extraordinary talents, to

whom, without ever becoming attached, he had become accustomed. His remark on the event is full of his fine reserve and sobriety of feeling : " You have doubtless heard of the loss I have had in Dr. Middleton, whose house was the only easy place one could find to converse in at Cambridge. For my part I find a friend so uncommon a thing, that I cannot help regretting even an old acquaintance, which is an indifferent likeness of it, and though I don't approve the spirit of his books, methinks 'tis pity the world should lose so rare a thing as a good writer."

In the same letter he tells Wharton that he himself is neither cheerful nor easy in bodily health, and yet has the mortification to find his spiritual part the most infirm thing about him. He is applying himself heartily to the study of zoology, and has procured for that purpose the works of M. de Buffon. In reply to Wharton's urgent entreaties for a visit, he agrees that he " could indeed wish to refresh my ἐνεργέια a little at Durham by a sight of you, but when is there a probability of my being so happy ?" However, it seems that he would have contrived this expedition, had it not been for the aforesaid cousin, Mrs. Forster, " a person as strange, and as much to seek, as though she had been born in the mud of the Ganges." At the same time he warns Wharton against returning to Cambridge, saying that Mrs. Wharton will find life very dreary in a place where women are so few, and those " squeezy and formal, little skilled in amusing themselves or other people. All I can say is, she must try to make up for it among the men, who are not over agreeable neither."

In spite of this warning, the Whartons appear to have come back to Cambridge. At all events we find Dr. Wharton wavering between that town and Bath as the

best place for him to practise in as a physician, and there-
upon there follows a gap of two years in Gray's correspondence with him.   The affectionate familiarity of the poet
with both Dr. and Mrs. Wharton when they re-emerge in
his correspondence, the pet names he has for the children,
and the avuncular air of intimacy implied, make it almost
certain that in 1751 and 1752 he had the pleasure of seeing these dear friends settled at his side, and enjoyed in
their family circle the warmth and brightness of a home.
At all events, after the publication of the *Elegy*, Gray is
once more lost to us for two years, most unaccountably,
since, if the Whartons were close beside him, and Mason
across the street at Pembroke, Walpole all this time was
exercising his vivacious and importunate pen at Strawberry Hill, and trying to associate Gray in all his schemes
and fancies.

One of Walpole's sudden whims was a friendship for
that eccentric and dissipated person, Richard Bentley, only
son of the famous Master of Trinity, whose acquaintance
Walpole made in 1750.   This man was an amateur artist
of more than usual talent, an elegant scholar in his way,
and with certain frivolous gifts of manner that were alter-
nately pleasing and displeasing to Walpole.   The artistic
merit of Bentley was exaggerated in his own time and has
been underrated since, nor does there now exist any important relic of it except his designs for Gray's poems.   In
the summer of 1752 Horace Walpole seems to have
suggested to Dodsley the propriety of publishing an *édition
de luxe* of Gray, with Bentley's illustrations; but as early
as June 1751 these illustrations were being made.   As
Gray gave the poems for nothing, and as Walpole paid
Bentley to draw and Müller to engrave the illustrations,
it is not surprising that Dodsley was eager to close with

the offer.   Bentley threw himself warmly into the project;
it is quite certain that he consulted Gray step by step, for
the designs show an extraordinary attention to the details
and even to the hints of the text.   Most probably the
three gentlemen amused themselves during the long vacation of 1752 by concocting the whole thing together.
Gray who, it must be remembered, was a connoisseur in
painting, was so much impressed by Bentley's talent and
versatility, that he addressed to him a copy of beautiful
verses, which, unfortunately existed only in a single
manuscript, and had been torn before Mason found them.
In these he says :—

> The tardy rhymes that used to linger on,
>   To censure cold, and negligent of fame,
> In swifter measures animated run,
>   And catch a lustre from his genuine flame.
>
> Ah! could they catch his strength, his easy grace,
>   His quick creation, his unerring line,
> The energy of Pope they might efface,
>   And Dryden's harmony submit to mine.
>
> But not to one in this benighted age
>   Is that diviner inspiration given,
> That burns in Shakespeare's or in Milton's page,
>   The pomp and prodigality of heaven.
>
> As when conspiring in the diamond's blaze,
>   The meaner gems that singly charm the sight,
> Together dart their intermingled rays,
>   And dazzle with a luxury of light.

This is the Landorian manner of praising, and almost
the only instance of a high note of enthusiasm in the
entire writings of Gray.   Bentley was not ludicrously
unworthy of such eulogy; his designs are extremely
remarkable in their way.   In an age entirely given up to

composed and conventional forms, he seems to have drawn
from nature and to have studied the figure from life.

Early in March, 1753, the Poemata-Grayo-Bentleiana, as
Walpole called them, appeared, a small thin folio, on very
thick paper, printed only on one side, and entitled, *Designs
by Mr. R. Bentley for Six Poems by Mr. T. Gray.* This
is the *editio princeps* of Gray's collected poems, and consists of the *Ode to Spring* (here simply called *Ode*), and
of the *Ode on the death of a Favourite Cat*, of both of
which it was the second edition ; a third edition of the
Eton Ode ; a first appearance of *A Long Story* and *Hymn
to Adversity ;* and a twelfth edition of the *Elegy written in
a Country Churchyard.* Bentley's illustrations consist of
a frontispiece, and a full-page design for each poem, with
headpieces, tailpieces, and initial letters. The frontispiece
is a border of extremely ingenious rococo ornament sur-
rounding a forest-glade, in which Gray, a graceful little
figure, sits in a pensive attitude. This has a high value
for us, since to any one accustomed to the practice of art,
it is obvious that this is a sketch from life, not a composed
study, and we have here in all probability a portrait of
the poet in his easiest attitude. The figure is that of a
young man, of small stature, but elegantly made, with a
melancholy and downcast countenance.

The portraiture becomes still more certain when we turn
to the indiscreet, but extremely interesting design for *A Long
Story*, where we not only have a likeness of Gray in 1753
which singularly resembles the more elaborate portrait of
him painted by Eckhardt in 1747, but we have also Lady
Schaub, Mr. Purt, and, what is most interesting of all, the
pretty delicate features of Miss Speed. The Rev. Mr.
Purt is represented as blowing the trumpet of Fame, while
the amazon ladies fly through the air, seeking for their

victim the poet, who is being concealed by the Muses
otherwhere than in a gorge of Parnassus. The designs
are engraved on copper by two well-known men of that
day. The best are by John Sebastian Müller, some of
whose initial letters are simply exquisite in execution;
the rest are the work of a man of greater reputation in
that day, Charles Grignion, whose work in this instance
lacks the refinement of Müller's, which is indeed of a very
high order. Grignion was the last survivor among persons
associated with the early and middle life of Gray; he
lived to be nearly a hundred years old, and died as late
as 1810. It might be supposed that the merits of the
designs to the *Six Poems* lay in the interpretation given
by engravers of so much talent to poor drawings, but we
happen to possess Gray's implicit statement that this was
not the case. If, therefore, we are to consider Bentley
responsible, for instance, for such realistic forms as the
nude figures in the head-piece to the *Hymn to Adversity*,
or for such feeling for foliage as is shown in the head and
tail pieces to the first ode, we must claim for him a higher
place in English art than has hitherto been conceded to
him. At all events the *Six Poems* of 1753 is one of the
few really beautiful books produced from an English press
during the middle of the eighteenth century, and in spite
of its rococo style, it is still a desirable possession.

It is pleasant to think of Gray reclining in the blue parlour over the supper-room at Strawberry Hill, turning over
prints with Horace Walpole, and glancing down the
garden to the Thames that flashed in silver behind the
syringas and honeysuckles; or seated, with a little touch
of sententious gravity, in the Library, chiding Chute and
their host for their frivolous taste in heraldry, or incited
by the dark panels and the old brass grate to chat of

architecture and decoration, and the new-found mysteries
of Gothic.   It is perhaps pleasanter still to think of him
dreaming in the garden of Stoke Pogis, or chatting over
a dish of tea with his old aunts, as he called his mother
and his aunt collectively, or strolling, with a book in his
hand, along the southward ridge of meadows to pay Lady
Cobham a stately call, or flirt a little with Miss Harriet
Speed.

But this quietude was not to last much longer.   Walpole, indeed, was surprised to have a visit from him in
January, 1753, just when Bentley's prints were going to
press, for Gray had been suddenly called up from Cambridge to Stoke by the news of his mother's illness.   He
had not expected to find her alive, but when he arrived
she was much better, and remained so for more than a
month.   He did not choose, however, to leave her, and
was at Stoke when the proof of Bentley's *cul-de-lampe* for
the *Elegy* arrived ; this represents a village-funeral, and
being examined by the old ladies, was conceived by them
to be a burying-ticket.   They asked him whether anybody
had left him a ring ; and hereupon follows a remark which
shows that Gray had never mentioned to his mother or
either of his aunts that he wrote verses ; nor would now
do so, lest they should " burn me for a poet."   A week or
two later, Walpole and Gray very nearly had another
quarrel.   Walpole, in his officiousness, had had Eckhardt's
portrait of Gray, which hung in the library at Strawberry
Hall, engraved for the *Six Poems*, a step which, taken as
it was without the poet's cognizance, drew down on Walpole an excessively sharp letter—" Gray does not hate to
find fault with me "—and a final veto on any such parade
of personality.

Mrs. Gray soon ceased to rally, and after a painful

struggle for life, expired on the 11th of March, 1753, at
the age of sixty-seven. Her son saw her buried, in the
family tomb, on the south side of the church-yard, near the
church, where may still be read the exquisitely simple and
affecting epitaph which he inscribed on her tombstone :—

In the same pious confidence, beside her friend and sister,
here sleep the remains of Dorothy Gray, widow, the careful
tender mother of many children, one of whom alone had the
misfortune to survive her.

When, a few months later, Mason had been standing by the
death-bed of his father, and spoke to his friend of the awe
that he experienced, Gray's thoughts went back to his mother,
and he wrote :—"I have seen the scene you describe,
and know how dreadful it is : I know too I am the better
for it. We are all idle and thoughtless things, and have
no sense, no use in the world any longer than that sad impression lasts ; the deeper it is engraved the better."
These are the words which came into Byron's memory
when he received the news of his mother's death.

The Whartons had by this time returned to Durham, and
thither at last, in the autumn of 1753, Gray resolved to
visit them. He had been unable to remain at Stoke now
that it was haunted by the faces of the dead that he had
loved, and he went into those lodgings over the hosier's
shop in the eastern part of Jermyn Street, which were his
favourite haunt in London. He left town for Cambridge
in May, and in June wrote to Wharton to say that he was
at last going to set out with Stonehewer in a post-chaise
for the north. In the middle of July they started, pro-
ceeding leisurely by Belvoir, Burleigh, and York, taking a
week to reach Studley. The journey was very agreeable,
and every place on the route which offered anything

curious in architecture, the subject at this moment most in Gray's thoughts, was visited and described in the note-book. Gray remained for two whole months and more in Dr. Wharton's house at Durham, associating with the bishop, Dr. Trevor, and having "one of the most beautiful vales in England to walk in, with prospects that change every ten steps, and open something new wherever I turn me, all rude and romantic." It had been proposed that on the return journey he should visit Mason at Hull, but the illness of that gentleman's father prevented this scheme, and the friends met at York instead. Gray travelled southwards for two days with "a Lady Swinburne, a Roman Catholic, not young, that has been much abroad, seen a great deal, knew a great many people, very chatty and communicative, so that I passed my time very well." I regret that the now-living and illustrious descendant of this amusing lady is unable to tell me anything definite of her history.

Gray came back to Cambridge to find the lime-trees changing colour, stayed there one day, and was just preparing to proceed to his London lodgings, when an express summoned him to Stoke, where his aunt Mrs. Rogers had suffered a stroke of the palsy. He arrived on the 6th of October, to find everything "resounding with the wood-lark and robin, and the voice of the sparrow heard in the land." His aunt, who was in her seventy-eighth year, had rallied to a surprising degree, and her recovery was not merely temporary. It would seem from an expression in one of his letters, that his paternal aunt, Mrs. Oliffe, had now gone down from Norwich to Stoke, to live with Mrs. Rogers. I do not remember that the history of literature presents us with the memoirs of any other poet favoured by nature with so many aunts as Gray possessed. Stoke was not a home for Gray with Mrs. Rogers bed-

I

ridden and with Mrs. Oliffe for its other inmate. The
hospitable Whartons seem again to have taken pity on
him, and he went from Jermyn Street up to Durham to
spend with them Christmas of this same year, 1753.

Walpole remarked that Gray was "in flower" during
these years 1750—1755. It was the blossoming of a
shrub which throws out only one bud each season, and
that bud sometimes nipped by an untimely frost. The
rose on Gray's thorn for 1754 was an example of these
blighted flowers, that never fully expanded. The *Ode on
Vicissitude*, which was found after the poet's death, in a
pocket-book of that year, should have been one of his
finest productions, but it is unrevised and hopelessly
truncated. Poor Mason rushed in where a truer poet
might have feared to tread, and clipped the straggling
lines, and finished it; six complete stanzas, however,
are the genuine work of Gray. The verse-form has a
catch in the third line, which is perhaps the most
delicate metrical effect Gray ever attained; while some
of the nature-painting in the poem is really exquisite.

> New-born flocks, in rustic dance,
>   Frisking ply their feeble feet;
> Forgetful of their wintry trance,
>   The birds his presence greet:
> But chief the sky-lark warbles high
> His trembling thrilling ecstasy,
> And, lessening from the dazzled sight,
> Melts into air and liquid light.

Here is a stanza which might almost be Wordsworth's :—

> See the wretch, that long has tost
>   On the thorny bed of pain,
> At length repair his vigour lost,
>   And breathe and walk again:

> The meanest floweret of the vale,
> The simplest note that swells the gale,
> The common sun, the air, the skies,
> To him are opening paradise.

That graceful trifler with metre, the sprightly Gresset, had written an *Epitre à ma Sœur* to which Gray frankly avowed that he owed the idea of his poem on Vicissitude. But it was only a few commonplaces which the English poet borrowed from the French one, who might, indeed, remind him that—

> Mille spectacles, qu'autrefois
> On voyait avec nonchalance,
> Transportent aujourd'hui, présentant des appas
> Inconnus à l'indifférence,

but was quite incapable of Gray's music and contemplative felicities. This *Ode on Vicissitude* seems, in some not very obvious way, to be connected with the death of Pope. It is possible that these were the " few autumn verses " which Gray began to write on that occasion. His manner of composition, his slow, half-hearted, desultory touch, his whimsical fits of passing inspiration, are unique in their kind ; there never was a professional poet whose mode was so thoroughly that of the amateur.

A short prose treatise, first printed in 1814, and named by the absurd Mathias *Architectura Gothica*, although the subject of it is purely Norman architecture, seems to belong to this year 1754. Gray was the first man in England to understand architecture scientifically, and his taste was simply too pure to be comprehended in an age that took William Kent for its architectural prophet. Even among those persons of refined feeling who desired to cultivate a taste for old English buildings, there was a sad absence of exact knowledge. Akenside thought that

the ruins of Persepolis formed a beautiful example of the
Gothic style ; and we know that Horace Walpole dazzled his
contemporaries with the gimcrack pinnacles of Strawberry
Hill. We may see from Bentley's frontispiece to the
Elegy, where a stucco moulding is half torn away, and
reveals a pointed arch of brick-work, that even among the
elect the true principles of Gothic architecture were
scarely understood. What Georgian amateurs really
admired was a grotto with cockle-shells and looking-glass,
such as the Greatheads made at Guy's Cliff, or such
follies in foliage as Shenstone perpetrated at Leasowes.
Gray strove hard to clear his memory of all such trifling,
and to arm his reason against arguments such as those of
Pococke, who held that the Gothic arch was a degradation
of the Moorish cupola, or of Batty Langley, who invented
five orders in a new style of his own. Gray's treatise on
Norman architecture is so sound and learned that it is
much to be regretted that he has not left us more of his
architectural essays. He formed his opinions from personal observation and measurement. Among the Pembroke MSS. there are copious notes of a tour in the Fens,
during which he jotted down the characteristics of all
the principal minsters, as far as Crowland and Boston.
It is not too much to say that Gray was the first modern
student of the history of architecture. Norton Nicholls
has recorded that when certain would-be people of taste
were wrangling about the style in which some ancient
building was constructed, Gray cut the discussion short
by saying, in the spirit of Mr. Ruskin, " Call it what you
please, but allow that it is beautiful." He did not
approve of Walpole's Gothic constructions at Strawberry
Hill, and frankly told him, when he was shown the gilding
and the glass, that he had " degenerated into finery."

CHAPTER VI.

It is not known at what time Gray resolved on composing poems which should resemble in stanzaic structure the triumphal odes or *epinikia* of Pindar, but it is certain that towards the close of 1754 he completed one such elaborate lyric. On the 26th of December of that year he gave the finishing touches to an "ode in the Greek manner," and sent it from Cambridge to Dr. Wharton, with the remark, "If this be as tedious to you as it is grown to me, I shall be sorry that I sent it you. . . . . I desire you would by no means suffer this to be copied, nor even show it, unless to very few, and especially not to mere scholars, that can scan all the measures in Pindar, and say the scholia by heart." Months later, Mason was pleading for a copy, but in vain. The poem thrown off so indifferently was that now known to us as *The Progress of Poesy*, and it marked a third and final stage in Gray's poetical development. In the early odes he had written for his contemporaries; in the *Elegy in a Country Churchyard* he had written for all the world; in the Pindaric Odes he was now to write for poets. In the *Elegy* he had dared to leave those trodden paths of phraseology along which the critics of the hour, the quibbling Hurds and Warburtons, could follow him step by step, but his startling felicities had carried his readers captive by their appeal to a common humanity. He was now about to launch upon a manner of writing in which he could no longer be accompanied by the plaudits of the vulgar, and where his style could no longer appeal with security to the sympathy of the critics. He was now, in other words, about to put out his most original qualities in poetry.

That he could not hope for popularity, he was aware at the outset ; "be assured," he consoled his friends, "that my taste for praise is not like that of children for fruit ; if there were nothing but medlars and blackberries in the world, I could be very well content to go without any at all ;" he could wait patiently for the suffrage of his peers. The very construction of the poem was a puzzle to his friends, although it is one of the most intelligibly and rationally built of all the odes in the language. It is in point of fact, a poem of three stanzas, in an elaborately consistent verse-form, with forty-one lines in each stanza. The length of these periods is relieved by the regular division of each stanza into strophe, antistrophe, and epode, the same plan having been used by no previous English poet but Congreve, who had written in 1705 a learned and graceful *Discourse on the Pindarique Ode*, which Gray was possibly acquainted with. Congreve's practice, however, had been as unsatisfactory as his theory was excellent, and Gray was properly the first poet to comprehend and follow the mode of Pindar.

Mr. Matthew Arnold has pointed out that the evolution of *The Progress of Poesy* is no less noble and sound than its style. It is worthy of remark that the power of evolution has not been common among lyrical poets even of a high rank. Even in Milton it is strangely absent, and we feel that all his odes, beautiful as they are, do not bud and branch and fall in fruit, closing with the exhaustion of their functions, but merely cease, because all poems must stop somewhere. The *Nativity Ode* does not close because the poet has nothing more to say, but merely because " 'tis time our tedious song should here have ending." In Collins, surely, we find the same failing ; the poem is a burst of emotion, but not an organism. The much-lauded *Ode to Liberty*, with its opening peal of trumpet-music, ends with a foolish abruptness, as if the poet had got tired of his instrument, and had thrown it away. Shelley, again, in his longer odes, seems to lose himself in beautiful meandering oratory, and to stop, as he began, in response to a mere change of purpose. Keats, on the other hand, is always consistent in his evolution, and so is Wordsworth at his more elevated moments ; the same may even be remarked of a poet infinitely below these in intellectual value, Edgar Poe. Gray, however, is the main example in our literature of a poet possessing this Greek quality of structure in his lyrical work, and it is to be noted that throughout his career it never left him, even on occasions when he was deserted by every other form of inspiration. His poems, whatever they are, are never chains of consecutive stanzas ; each line, each group of lines, has its proper place in a structure that could not be shorter or longer without a radical re-arrangement of ideas.

The strophe of the opening stanza of *The Progress of Poesy* invokes that lyre of Æolian strings, the breathings of those Æolian flutes, which Pindar had made the symbol of the art of poetry, and the sources, progress, and various motion of that art, " enriching every subject with a pomp of diction and luxuriant harmony of numbers," are described under the image of a thousand descending streams.

The antistrophe returns to the consideration of the power
of poetry, not now in motion, but an alluring and a sooth-
ing force around which the Passions throng and are subdued, a thought being here borrowed apparently from
Collins; the epode continues and combines these two
strains of thought, and shows that poetry, whether in
motion or at rest, is working the good will of Love, who
deigns herself to move in a rhythmic harmony, and be the
slave of verse.   In the second stanza, the strophe recalls
the miserable state of man, relieved by the amenities of
the heavenly Muse, who arms Hyperion against the sickly
company of Night; the antistrophe shows us how the
need of song arose in savage man, and illuminated "their
feather-cinctured chiefs, and dusky loves;" while the epode
breaks into an ecstatic celebration of the advent of poetic
art to Greece :—

> Woods, that wave o'er Delphi's steep,
> Isles, that crown th' Ægean deep,
>   Fields, that cool Ilissus laves,
>   Or where Mæander's amber waves
> In lingering labyrinths creep,
>   How do your tuneful echoes languish,
>   Mute, but to the voice of anguish!
> Where each old poetic mountain
>   Inspiration breathed around;
> Every shade and hallowed fountain
>   Murmured deep a solemn sound.

But the Muses, "in Greece's evil hour," went to Rome,
and "when Latium had her lofty spirit lost," it was to
Albion that they turned their steps.   The third strophe
describes how the awful Mother unveiled her face to
Shakespeare; the antistrophe celebrates the advent of
Milton and Dryden, while the final epode winds the whole
poem to a close with a regret that the lyre once held by

the last-named poet has degenerated into hands like
Gray's :—

> Hark! his hands the lyre explore!
> Bright-eyed Fancy, hovering o'er,
> Scatters from her pictured urn
> Thoughts that breathe, and words that burn.
> But ah! 'tis heard no more—
> Oh! lyre divine, what daring spirit
> Wakes thee now?   Though he inherit
> Not the pride, nor ample pinion,
>   That the Theban eagle bear,
> Sailing with supreme dominion
>   Thro' the azure deep of air :
> Yet oft before his infant eyes would run
>   Such forms as glitter in the Muse's ray,
> With orient hues, unborrowed of the sun:
>   Yet shall he mount, and keep his distant way
> Beyond the limits of a vulgar fate,
> Beneath the Good how far,—but far above the Great.

In these passages, especially where he employs the double
rhyme, we seem to catch in Gray the true modern accent,
the precursor of the tones of Shelley and Byron, both of
whom, but especially the former, were greatly influenced
by this free and ringing music.   The reader has only to
compare the epode last quoted with the choruses in *Hellas*
to see what Shelley owed to the science and invention of
Gray.   This manner of rhyming, this rapid and recurrent
beat of song, was the germ out of which have sprung all
later metrical inventions, and without which Mr. Swinburne himself might now be polishing the heroic
couplet to its last perfection of brightness and sharp-
ness.

Another Pindaric ode on *The Liberty of Genius* was
planned about the same time, but of this there exists only
the following fragment of an argument :—" All that men

of power can do for men of genius is to leave them at their
liberty, compared to birds that, when confined to a cage,
do but regret the loss of their freedom in melancholy
strains, and lose the luscious wildness and happy luxuriance of their notes, which used to make the woods
resound." The subject is one well-fitted to its author's
power, and we regret its loss as we regret that of Collins'
Ode on the Music of the Grecian Theatre. Unlike that
blue rose of the bibliophiles, however, Gray's ode probably
was never written at all.

In the meantime not much was happening to Gray
himself. His friend Mason had taken holy orders, and in
November 1754 had become rector of Aston and chap-
lain to the Earl of Holdernesse ; "we all are mighty glad,"
says Gray, "that he is in orders, and no better than any
of us." Early in 1755 both Mason and Walpole set upon
Gray to publish a new volume of poems, whereupon he
held up the single ode *On the Progress of Poesy*, and asked
if they wished him to publish a "little sixpenny flam"
like that, all by itself. He threatened if Wharton be tiresome, since the publishing faction had gained him over to
their side, to write an ode against physicians, with some
very stringent lines about magnesia and alicant soap.
Pembroke meanwhile had just received an undergraduate
of quality, Lord Strathmore, Thane of Glamis, "a tall,
genteel figure" that pleased Gray, and presently was
admitted within the narrow circle of his friends.

According to Mason, the exordium of the *Bard* was completed in March 1755, having occupied Gray for about three
months. In the case of this very elaborate poem, Gray
seems to have laid aside his customary reticence, and to have
freely consulted his friends. Mason had seen the beginning
of it before he went to Germany in May of that year, when

he found in Hamburg a literary lady who had read the
"*Nitt Toats*" of Young, and thought the *Elegy in a
Country Church-Yard* "bien jolie et mélancholique." Mason
at Hanover meets Lord Nuneham, and is sure that Gray
would delight in him, because he is so peevish and sensible
and so good a hater, which gives us a passing glance at
Gray himself. *The Bard* was exactly two years and five
months in reaching completion, and the slowness of its
growth was the subject of mirth with Gray himself, who
called it "Odikle," and made fun of its stunted propor-
tions.

On the 15th of July, 1755, Gray went down to the Vine,
in Hampshire, to visit his old friend Chute, who was now
beginning to recover a little from the shock of the death
of his beloved heir and nephew. In the congenial company of the Italianate country gentleman Gray stayed a
few days, and then went on to Southampton, Winchester,
Portsmouth, and Netley Abbey, returning to Stoke on the
31st of July. Unfortunately he either took a chill on this
little tour, or overtaxed his powers, and from this time to
the end of his life, a period of sixteen years, he was
seldom in a condition of even tolerable health. In August
he was obliged to put himself under medical treatment;
one alarming attack of gout after the other continued to
undermine his constitution, and his system was further
depressed by an exhausting regimen of magnesia and salts
of wormwood. He had to lie up at Stoke for many weeks,
with aching feet and temples, and was bled until he was
too giddy and feeble to walk with comfort. All this
autumn and winter of 1755 his symptoms were very
serious. He could not sleep; he was troubled by a nervous deafness, and a pain in the region of the heart which
seldom left him. Meanwhile he did not leave *The Bard*

untouched, but progressed slowly with it, as though he were a sculptor, deliberately pointing and chiselling a statue. He adopted the plan of copying strophes and fragments of it in his letters, and many such scraps exist in MS. Late in the autumn, however, he thought that he was falling into a decline, and in a fit of melancholy he laid *The Bard* aside.

Gray was altogether in a very nervous, distracted condition at this time, and first began to show symptoms of that fear of fire, which afterwards became almost a mania with him, by desiring Wharton to insure the two houses, at Wanstead and in Cornhill, which formed a principal part of his income; from the amount of the policies of these houses, we can infer that the first was a property of considerable value. The death of his mother, following on that of Miss Antrobus, had, it may here be remarked, removed all pressure of poverty from Gray for the remainder of his life. He was never rich, but from this time forward he was very comfortably provided for. Horace Walpole appears to have been alarmed at his friend's condition of health, and planned a change of scene for him, which it seems unfortunate that he could not persuade himself to undertake. George Hervey, Earl of Bristol, was named English Minister at Lisbon, and he offered to take Gray with him as his secretary, but the proud little poet refused. Perhaps the climate of Portugal might have proved too relaxing for him, and he might have laid his bones beside that grave where the grass was hardly green yet over the body of Fielding.

Gray's terror of fire has already been alluded to, and it had now become so marked as to be a subject of conversation in the college. He professed rather openly to believe that some drunken fellow or other would burn the

college down about their heads.   On the 9th of January,
1756, he asked Dr. Wharton to buy him a rope-ladder of a
man in Wapping who advertised such articles.   It was to
be rather more than thirty-six feet long, with strong hooks
at the top.   This machine Wharton promptly forwarded,
and Gray proceeded to have an iron bar fixed within his
bedroom-window.   This bar, crossing a window which
looks towards Pembroke, still exists and marks Gray's
chambers at Peterhouse.   Such preparations, however, could
not be made without attracting great attention in the latter college, where Gray was by no means a favourite among
the high-coloured young gentlemen who went bull-baiting
to Heddington or came home drunk and roaring from a
cock-shying at Market Hill.   Accordingly the noisy fellow-
commoners determined to have a lark at the timid little
poet's expense, and one night in February 1756, when
Gray was asleep in bed, they suddenly alarmed him with
a cry of fire on his staircase, having previously placed a
tub of water under his window.   The ruse succeeded only
too well : Gray, without staying to put on his clothes,
hooked his rope-ladder to the iron bar, and descended
nimbly into the tub of water, from which he was rescued
with shouts of laughter by the unmannerly youths.   But
the jest might easily have proved fatal ; as it was, he
shivered in the February air so excessively that he had to
be wrapped in the coat of a passing watchman, and to be
carried into the college by the friendly Stonehewer, who
now appeared on the scene.   To our modern ideas this out-
rage on a harmless middle-aged man of honourable position,
who had done nothing whatever to provoke insult or
injury, is almost inconceivable.   But there was a deep
capacity for brutal folly underneath the varnish of the
eighteenth century, and no one seems to have sympathized

with Gray or to have thought the conduct of the youths ungentlemanly. As, when Dryden was beaten by Rochester's hired and masked bravos, it was felt that Dryden was thereby disgraced, so Gray's friends were consistently silent on this story, as though it were a shame to him, and we owe our knowledge of the particulars to strangers, more especially to a wild creature called Archibald Campbell, who actually ventured to tell the tale during Gray's life-time.

Gray was very angry, and called upon the authorities of his college to punish the offenders. Mason says: "After having borne the insults of two or three young men of fortune longer than might reasonably have been expected from a man of less warmth of temper, Mr. Gray complained to the governing part of the Society, and not thinking that his remonstrance was sufficiently attended to, quitted the College." He went over to his old friends at Pembroke,[1] who welcomed him with one accord as if he had been "Mary of Valens in person." Under the foundation of this sainted lady he remained for the rest of his life, comfortably lodged, surrounded by congenial friends, and "as quiet as in the Grande Chartreuse." He does not seem to have ever been appointed to a fellowship at Pembroke. The chambers he is supposed to have occupied are still shown, a large low room at the western end of the Hitcham Building, bright and pleasant, with windows looking east and west. He adopted habits at Pembroke which he had never indulged in at Peterhouse. He was the first, and for a long while the only person in the University who made his rooms look pretty. He took

[1] In the Admission-Book at Pembroke there is this entry: "Thomas Gray, LL.B., admissus est ex Collegio Divi Petro. March (*sic*) 6, 1756."

care that his windows should be always full of mignonette
or some other sweetly-scented plant, and he was famous
for a pair of huge Japanese vases, in blue and white china.
His servant, Stephen Hempstead, had to keep the room
as bright and spick as an old lady's bandbox, and not an
atom of dust was allowed to rest on the little harpsichord
where the poet used to sit in the twilight and play toc-
catas of Scarlatti or Pergolesi. Here for fifteen quiet
years, the autumn of his life, Gray lived among his books,
his china, and his pictures, and here at last we shall see
him die, with the good Master of Pembroke, *le Petit Bon
Homme*, holding his hand in the last services of friendship. Well might Gray write to Wharton (March 25th,
1756):—" Removing myself from Peterhouse to Pembroke
may be looked upon as a sort of æra in a life so barren of
events as mine."

Curiously enough, the shock and agitation of the scene
that has been just described appear to have had no ill
effect upon Gray's health. His letters at this time became,
on the contrary, much more buoyant in tone. In April
1756 an extraordinary concert of spiritual music, in which
the *Stabat Mater* of Pergolesi was for the first time given
in England, drew him up to London for three days,
during which time he lodged with Wharton. All the
ensuing summer Mason, now and henceforth known as
"Scroddles" in Gray's correspondence, was perpetrating
reams of poetry, or prose astonished out of its better nature
at the sudden invasion of its provinces by rhyme. A terrible tragedy of *Caractacus*, suggested by the yet-unfinished
Bard, with much blank-verse invocation of "Arviragus,
my bold, my breathless boy," belongs to this year 1756,
and can now be read only by a very patient student bent
on finding how nimble Mason could be in borrowing the

mere shell and outward echo of Gray's poetical perform-
ances.   The famous

> While through the west, where sinks the crimson day,
> Meek twilight slowly sails, and waves her banners gray.

which Gray pronounced "superlative," and which the
modern reader must admit to be pretty, belong also to this
year, and are to be found in an ode of Mason's, *To a
Friend*, in which occurs the first contemporary celebration
of a greater name in literature than his :—

> Through this still valley let me stray,
> Rapt in some strain of pensive GRAY,
> Whose lofty genius bears along
> The conscious dignity of Song ;
> And, scorning from the sacred store
> To waste a note on Pride or Power,
> Roves through the glimmering twilight gloom
> *And warbles round each rustic tomb :*
> He, too, perchance, (for well I know,
> His heart can melt with friendly woe)
> He, too, perchance, when these poor limbs are laid,
> Will heave one tuneful sigh, and sooth my hovering shade.

Gray must have smiled at this foolish tribute, but he
valued the affection that prompted it, and he deigned in a
fatherly way to beg Wharton to let him hear if these odes
were favourably spoken of in London.

The scene of Mason's *Caractacus* was laid in Mona, and
Gray was at this time engaged in the spiritual ascension of
Snowdon, with "Odikle" at his side.   "I hope we shall
be very good neighbours.   Any Druidical anecdotes that I
can meet with I will be sure to send you.   I am of opinion
that the ghosts "—for, alas ! there are ghosts in *Caractacus*
—" will spoil the picture, unless they are thrown at a huge
distance, and extremely kept down."   In June 1756

having "no more pores and muscular inflations, and troubled only with depression of mind," Gray at Stoke rather vaguely proposed to Mason at Tunbridge that they should spend the summer together on the Continent. "Shall we go in time, and have a house together in Switzerland? It is a fine poetical country to look at, and nobody there will understand a word we say or write." Mason was probably too much a child of his age to relish going to Switzerland; moreover, there was a chaplaincy to Lord John Cavendish towards which Mason was extending a greedy finger and thumb, and he preferred to remain in the happy hunting-grounds of endowment. Gray laughed with indulgent contempt at his young friend's grasping wishes, though when this intense desire for place passed all decent limits, he could reprove it sharply enough. To the sober and self-respecting Gray, who had never asked for anything in his life, to intrigue for church-preferment was the conduct of a child or a knave, and he accordingly persisted in treating Mason as a child.

Very little progress was made with *The Bard* in 1756. In December of that year "Odikle is not a bit grown, though it is fine mild open weather." Suddenly in May 1757 it was brought to a conclusion in consequence of some concerts given at Cambridge by John Parry, the famous blind harper, who lived until 1782, and whose son was one of the first A.R.A.'s. Gray's account of the extraordinary effect that this man's music made on him is expressed in that light vein with which he loved to conceal deep emotion. "There is no faith in man, no, not in a Welshman; and yet Mr. Parry has been here, and scratched out such ravishing blind harmony, such tunes of a thousand years old, with names enough to choke you, as have set all this learned body a dancing, and inspired them with due

K

reverence for my old Bard his countryman, wherever he
shall appear.   Mr. Parry, you must know, has put my Ode
in motion again, and has brought it at last to a conclusion.
'Tis to him, therefore, that you owe the treat which I send
you enclosed ; namely, the breast and merry-thought, and
rump too of the chicken which I have been chewing
so long, that I would give it to the world for neck-beef or
cow-heel."

The Ode so rudely spoken of is no less than that *Bard*
which for at least a century remained almost without a
rival among poems cherished by strictly poetical persons
for the qualities of sublimity and pomp of vision.   It is
only in the very latest generation, and among a school of
extremely refined critics that the ascendency of this ode
has been questioned, and certain pieces by Collins and
even by Blake preferred to it.   There is a great and even
a legitimate pleasure in praising that which plainly possesses very high merit, and which has too long been overlooked or neglected ; but we must beware of the paradox
which denies beauty in a work of art, *because* beauty has
always been discovered there.   Gray's *Bard* has enjoyed
an instant and sustained popularity, while Collins' noble
Ode to Liberty has had few admirers and Blake's *Book of
Thel* till lately has had none ; but there is no just reason
why a wish to assert the value of the patriotic fervour of
the one poem and the rosy effusion of the other should
prevent us from acknowledging that, great as are the
qualities of these pieces, the human sympathy, historical
imagination, and sustained dithyrambic dignity of *The
Bard* are also great, and probably greater.   All that has
been said of the evolution of the *Progress of Poesy* is true
of that of *The Bard*, while those attributes which our old
critics used to term "the machinery" are even more bril-

liant and appropriate in the longer poem than in the shorter.
In form the poems are sufficiently analogous; each has
three main divisions, with strophe, antistrophe, and epode,
and in each the epode is dedicated to briskly rhyming
measures and experiments in metre. The opening is admirably startling and effective; the voice that meets us
with its denunciations is that of the last survivor of the
ancient race of Celtic bards, a venerable shape who is
seated on a rock above the defile through which the forces
of Edward I. are about to march. This mysterious being,
in Gray's own words, "with a voice more than human,
reproaches the king with all the misery and desolation
which he had brought on his country; foretells the mis-
fortunes of the Norman race, and with prophetic spirit
declares, that all his cruelty shall never extinguish the
noble ardour of poetic genius in this island; and that men
shall never be wanting to celebrate true virtue and valour
in immortal strains, to expose vice and infamous pleasure,
and boldly censure tyranny and oppression." The scheme
of the poem, therefore, is strictly historical, and yet is not
very far removed from that of Gray's previous written and
unwritten Pindaric odes. In these three poems, the dignity of genius and its function as a ruler and benefactor
of mankind are made the chief subject of discourse, and a
mission is claimed for artists in verse than which none was
ever conceived more brilliant or more august. But, fortunately for his readers, Gray was diverted from his purely
abstract consideration of history into a concrete observation
of its most picturesque forms, and forgot to trace the
"noble ardour of poetic genius" in painting vivid pictures
of Edward II. enduring his torture in Berkeley Castle,
and of the massacre of the bards at the battle of Camlan.
Some of the scenes which pass across the magic mirror

of the old man's imagination are unrivalled for concision
and force. That in which the court of Elizabeth, surrounded by her lords and her poets, flashes upon the
inner eye, is of an inimitable felicity :—

> Girt with many a baron bold,
> Sublime their starry fronts they rear;
>   And gorgeous dames, and statesmen old
> In bearded majesty, appear;
> In the midst a form divine!
> Her eye proclaims her of the Briton-line;
> Her lion-port, her awe-commanding face,
> Attempered sweet to virgin-grace.
> What strings symphonious tremble in the air,
>   What strains of vocal transport round her play.
> Hear from the grave, great Taliessin, hear;
>   They breathe a soul to animate thy clay.
> Bright Rapture calls, and soaring as she sings,
> Waves in the eye of heaven her many-coloured wings.

This closing vision of a pretty but incongruous "Rapture" may remind us that the crowning fault of Gray and
his school, their assumption that a mythology might be
formed out of the emotions of the human mind, and a new
Olympus be fitted out with brand-new gods of a moralist's
making, is rarely prominent in *The Bard* or the *Elegy in a
Country Churchyard*, his two greatest works. Some use
of allegorical abstraction is necessary to the very structure
of poetry, and is to be found in the works of our most
realistic writers. It is in its excess that it becomes ridiculous or tedious, as in Mason and other imitators of Gray.
The master himself was not by any means able at all times
to clothe his abstractions with flesh and blood, but he is
never ridiculous. He felt, indeed, the danger of the tendency in himself and others, and he made some remarks
on the subject to Mason which were wholly salutary :—

I had rather some of these personages, "Resignation,"
"Peace," "Revenge," "Slaughter," "Ambition," were
stripped of their allegorical garb. A little simplicity here and
there in the expression would better prepare the high and fantastic strain, and all the imaginable harpings that follow. . . .
The true lyric style, with all its flights of fancy, ornaments, and
heightening of expression, and harmony of sound, is in its
nature superior to every other style; which is just the cause
why it could not be borne in a work of great length, no more
than the eye could bear to see all this scene that we constantly
gaze upon,—the verdure of the fields and woods, the azure of
the sea and skies, turned into one dazzling expanse of gems.
The epic, therefore, assumed a style of graver colours, and only
stuck on a diamond (borrowed from her sister) here and there,
where it best became her. When we pass from the diction that
suits this kind of writing to that which belongs to the former,
it appears natural, and delights us : but to pass on a sudden
from the lyric glare to the epic solemnity (if I may be allowed to
talk nonsense) has a very different effect. We seem to drop
from verse into mere prose, from light into darkness. Do you
not think if Mingotti stopped in the middle of her best air, and
only repeated the remaining verses (though the best Metastasio
ever wrote) that they would not appear very cold to you, and
very heavy ?

Between Dryden and Wordsworth there was no man
but Gray who could write in prose about his art with such
coherence and science as this. These careless sentences
outweigh tomes of Blair's glittering rhetoric and Hurd's
stilted disquisitions on the Beautiful and the Elevated.

Almost directly after Gray had finished *The Bard* he
was called upon to write an epitaph for a lady, Mrs. Jane
Clarke, who had died in childbirth at Epsom, where her
husband was a physician, on the 27th of April, 1757.
Dr. Clarke had been an early college friend of Gray's, and
he applied to Gray to write a copy of verses to be inscribed

on a tablet in Beckenham Church, where his wife was
buried. Gray wrote sixteen lines, not in his happiest
vein, and these found their way into print after his death.
In his tiny nosegay there is perhaps no flower so inconsiderable as this perfunctory *Epitaph*. One letter, several
years later than the date of this poem, proves that Gray
continued to write on intimate terms to Dr. Clarke, who
does not seem to have preserved the poet's correspondence,
and is not otherwise interesting to us. In April Gray
made another acquaintance, of a very different kind;
Lord Nuneham, a young man of fashion and fortune,
with a rage for poetry, came rushing down upon him with
a letter of introduction and a profusion of compliments.
He brought a large bouquet of jonquils, which he presented
to the poet with a reverence so profound that Gray could
not fail to smell the jessamine-powder in his periwig, and
indeed he was too fine " even for me," says the poet, " who
love a little finery." Lord Nuneham came expressly in
Newmarket week to protest against going to Newmarket,
and sat devoutly at Gray's feet, half fop, half enthusiast,
for three whole days, talking about verses and the fine
arts. Gray was quite pleased with him at last; and so
"we vowed eternal friendship, embraced, and parted."
Lord John Cavendish, too, was in Cambridge at this time,
and also pleased Gray, though in a very different and less
effusive manner.

In the summer of 1757 Horace Walpole set up a
printing-press at Strawberry Hill, and persuaded Gray to
let his Pindaric Odes be the first issue of the establish-
ment. Accordingly Gray sent him a MS. copy of the
poems, and they were set up with wonderful fuss and circumstance by Walpole's compositor; Gray being more
than usually often at Strawberry Hill this summer.

Dodsley agreed to publish the book, and 2000 copies were struck off. On the 29th of June Gray received forty guineas, the only money he ever gained by literature. On the 8th of August there was published a large thin quarto, entitled " *Odes* by Mr. Gray. Φωναντα συνετοισι. Printed at Strawberry Hill for R. and J. Dodsley in Pall Mall," with an engraving of Walpole's little gimcrack dwelling on the title-page. The two odes have no other titles than Ode I., Ode II.; they form a pamphlet of twenty-one pages, and were sold at one shilling. Small as the volume was, however, it was by no means insignificant, and it achieved a very great success. Garrick and Warburton led the chorus of praise; the famous actor publishing some verses in honour of the odes, the famous critic pronouncing them above the grasp of the public, and this indeed was true. In fact Gray lamented, as most men of genius have had to lament, that the praise he received was not always judicious praise, and therefore of little worth. " The Συνετοι," he says, " appear to be still fewer than even I expected." He became, however, a kind of lion. Goldsmith wrote an examination of the *Odes* for the *Monthly Review*. The Cobhams, at Stoke, were very civil, and Mr. and Mrs. Garrick came down there to stay with him ; the stiff, prim demeanour of Dr. Hurd melted into smiles and compliments ; the *Critical Review* was in raptures, though it mistook the Æolian Lyre for the Harp of Æolus ; and at York Races sporting peers were heard to discuss the odes in a spirit of bewildered eulogy. Within two months 1300 copies had been sold. Best of all, Miss Speed seemed to understand, and whispered " φωνᾶντα συνετοῖσι " in the most amiable and sympathetic tones. But Gray could enjoy nothing ; several little maladies hung over him, the general wreck of his frail

constitution began to be imminent.   Meanwhile small
things worried him.   The great Mr. Fox did not wonder
Edward I. could not understand what the Bard was saying, and chuckled at his own wit ; young Lord Nuneham,
for all his jonquils and his jessamine-powder, did not
trouble himself to acknowledge his presentation copy;
people said Gray's style was " impenetrable and inex-
plicable," and altogether the sweets were fewer than
the bitters in the cup of notoriety.

Gray had placed himself, however, at one leap at the
head of the living English poets.   Thomson and Blair
were now dead, Dyer was about to pass away, and Collins,
hopelessly insane, was making the cloisters of Chichester
resound with his terrible shrieks.   Young, now very aged,
had almost abandoned verse.   Johnson had retired from
all competition with the poets.   Smart, whose frivolous
verses had been collected in 1754, had shown himself, in
his few serious efforts, a direct disciple and imitator of
Gray's early style.   Goldsmith, Churchill, and Cowper
were still unheard of ; and the only men with whom
Gray could for a moment be supposed to contend were
Shenstone and Akenside.   Practically both of these men,
also, had retired from poetry, the latter indeed having
been silent for twelve years.   The *Odes* could hardly fail
to attract attention in a year which produced no other even
noticeable publication in verse, except Dyer's tiresome
descriptive poem of *The Fleece*.   Gray seems to have felt
that his genius, his " verve " as he called it, was trying
to breathe in a vacuum ; and from this time forward he
made even less and less effort to concentrate his powers.
In the winter of 1757, it is true, he began to plan
an epic or didactic poem on the Revival of Learning,
but we hear no more of it.   His few remaining poems

were to be lyrics, pure and simple, swallow-flights of song.

On the 12th of December, 1757, Colley Cibber died, having held the office of poet-laureate for twenty-seven years. Lord John Cavendish immediately suggested to his brother, the Duke of Devonshire, who was then Lord Chamberlain, that as Gray was the greatest living poet, the post should be offered to him. This was immediately done, in very handsome terms, the duke even offering to waive entirely the perfunctory writing of odes, which had hitherto been deemed an annual duty of all poets laureate. Gray directed Mason, through whom the offer had been made, to decline it very civilly :—

Though I well know the bland emollient saponaceous qualities both of sack and silver, yet if any great man would say to me "I make you Rat-catcher to his Majesty, with a salary of 300*l.* a-year and two butts of the best Malaga; and though it has been usual to catch a mouse or two, for form's sake, in public once a year, yet to you, sir, we shall not stand upon these things," I cannot say I should jump at it; nay if they would drop the very name of the office, and call me Sinecure to the King's Majesty, I should still feel a little awkward, and think everybody I saw smelt a rat about me; but I do not pretend to blame any one else that has not the same sensations; for my part I would rather be serjeant-trumpeter or pin-maker to the palace. Nevertheless, I interest myself a little in the history of it, and rather wish somebody may accept it that will retrieve the credit of the thing, if it be retrievable, or ever had any credit. Rowe was, I think, the last man of character that had it. As to Settle, whom you mention, he belonged to my lord mayor, not to the king. Eusden was a person of great hopes in his youth, though at last he turned out a drunken parson. Dryden was as disgraceful to the office, from his character, as the poorest scribbler could have been from his verses. The office itself has

always humbled the professor hitherto (even in an age when
kings were somebody), if he were a poor writer by making
him more conspicuous, and if he were a good one by setting
him at war with the little fry of his own profession, for there
are poets little enough to envy even a poet laureate.

The duke acted promptly, for within a week of Cibber's
death the laureateship had been offered to Gray, who
refused, and to Whitehead, who accepted it. This amiable
versifier was perhaps more worthy of the compliment
than Mason, who wished for it, and who raged with disappointment.

In January, 1758, Gray seems to have recovered sufficiently to be so busy buying South Sea annuities, and
amassing old china jars and three-legged stools with grass-
green bottoms, that he could not supply Mason with that
endless flood of comment on Mason's odes, tragedies, and
epics which the vivacious poetaster demanded. Hurd, in
the gentlemanly manner to which Mr. Leslie Stephen
has dedicated one stringent page, was calling upon Gray
to sympathize with him about the wickedness of " that
wretch " Akenside. In all this Gray had but slight
interest. His father's fortune, which had reached 10,000*l.*
in his mother's careful hands, had been much damaged by
the fire in Cornhill, and Gray now sank a large portion
of his property in an annuity, that he might enjoy a
larger income. During the spring of 1758 he amused
himself by writing in the blank leaves of Kitchen's English Atlas *A Catalogue of the Antiquities, Houses, &c., in
England and Wales*. This was considerable enough to
form a little volume, and in 1774, after Gray's death,
Mason printed a few copies of it privately, and sent them
round to Gray's friends ; and in 1787 issued a second
edition for sale.

In April of the same year, 1758, Dr. Wharton lost his eldest and at that time his only son. Gray not only wrote him a very touching letter of condolence, but some verses on the death of the child, which I first printed in 1885 from a MS. in the handwriting of Dyce. In May, Gray started on that architectural tour in the Fens, of which I have already spoken, and in June was summoned to Stoke by the illness of his aunt Mrs. Oliffe, who had a sort of paralytic stroke while walking in the garden. She recovered, however, and Gray returned to London, made a short stay at Hampton with Lord and Lady Cobham, and spent July at Strawberry Hill. In August the Garricks again visited him at Stoke, but he had hardly enough physical strength to endure their vivacity. "They are now gone, and I am not sorry for it, for I grow so old, that, I own, people in high spirits and gaiety overpower me, and entirely take away mine. I can yet be diverted by their sallies, but if they appear to take notice of my dullness, it sinks me to nothing. . . . I continue better than has been usual with me, in the summer, though I neither walk nor take anything : 'tis in mind only that I am weary and disagreeable." His position at Stoke, with Mrs. Oliffe laid up, and poor bed-ridden Mrs. Rogers growing daily weaker and weaker, was not an exhilarating one. Towards the end of September, Mrs. Rogers recovered her speech, which had for several years been almost unintelligible, flickered up for two or three days, and then died. She left Mrs. Oliffe joint executrix of her small property with Gray, who describes himself in November 1758 as "agreeably employed in dividing nothing with an old Harridan, who is the Spawn of Cerberus and the Dragon of Wantley." In January 1759 Mrs. Oliffe having taken herself off to her native country of Norfolk,

Gray closed the house at Stoke Pogis, and from this time forth only visited that village, which had been his home for nearly twenty years, when he was invited to stay at Stoke House. At the same time, to the distress of Dr. Brown, he ceased to reside at Pembroke, and spent the next three years in London.

CHAPTER VII.

WHEN the Sloane Collection became national property at the death of its founder in 1753, and was incorporated under an act which styled it the British Museum, scholars and antiquaries expected to enter at once upon their inheritance. But a site and a building had to be secured, and when these were discovered, it took a long while to fit up the commodious galleries of Montagu House. On the 15th of January, 1759, the Museum was thrown open to the public, and among the throng of visitors was Gray, who had settled himself and his household gods close by, in Southampton Row, and who for some weeks had been awaiting the official Sesame. He had been seeing something of London society meanwhile, — entertained by Lady Carlisle, invited to meet Rousseau, and attending concerts and plays. He gives some account of the performance of Metastasio's *Ciro Riconosciuto*, with Cocchi's agreeable music.

The British Museum he found "indeed a treasure." It was at first so crowded that "the corner room in the basement, furnished with a wainscot table and twenty chairs," was totally inadequate to supply the demand, and in order to be comfortable it was necessary to book a place a fortnight beforehand This pressure, however, only lasted for a very short time; curiosity was excited by the novelty, but quickly languished, and this little room was found quite ample enough to contain the scholars who frequented it. To reach it, the intrepid reader had to pass in darkness, like Jonah, through the belly of a whale, from which he emerged into the room of the Keeper of Printed Books, Dr. Peter Templeman, a physician who had received this responsible post for having translated *Norden's Travels*, and who resigned it, wearily, in 1761, for a more congenial appointment at the Society of Arts. By July 1759 the rush on the reading-room had entirely subsided, and on the ·23rd of that month Gray mentions to Mason that there are only five readers that day. These were Gray himself, Dr. Stukeley the antiquary, and three hack-writers who were copying MSS. for hire.

A little later on, Gray became an amused witness of those factions which immediately broke out among the staff of the British Museum, and which practically lasted until a very few years ago. People who were the diverted or regretful witnesses of dissensions between a late Principal Librarian and the scholars whom he governed may be consoled to learn that things were just as bad in 1759. Dr. Gawin Knight, the first Principal Librarian, a pompous martinet with no pretence to scholarship, made life so impossible to the keepers and assistants that the Museum was completely broken into a servile and a rebellious faction. Gray, moving noiselessly to and fro, noted all this and smiled; "the whole society, trustees and all, are up in arms, like the fellows of a college." Dr. Knight made no concessions; the keepers presently refused to salute him when they passed his window, and Gray and his fellow-readers were at last obliged to make a *détour* every day, because Dr. Knight had walled up a passage in order to annoy the keepers. Meanwhile the trustees were spending 500*l.* a year more than their income, and Gray confidently predicts that before long all the books and the crocodiles and Jonah's whale will be put up to public auction.

At Mr Jermyn's, in Southampton Row, Bloomsbury, Gray was very comfortably settled. It was a cleaner Bloomsbury than we know now, and a brighter. Gray from his bedroom-window looked out on a south-west garden-wall covered with flowering jessamine through June and July. There had been roses, too, in this London garden.· Gray must always have flowers about him, and he trudged down to Covent Garden every day, for his sweet peas and pinks, scarlet martagon-lilies, double stocks, and flowering marjoram. His drawing-room looked over Bedford Gardens, and a fine stretch of upland fields, crowned at last, against the sky, by the villages of Highgate and Hampstead. St. Giles's was at his back, with many a dirty court and alley, but in front of him against the morning light, there was little but sunshine and greenery and fresh air. He seems to notice nature here on the outskirts of London far more narrowly than at Cambridge; there are little parenthetical notes, asides to himself, about "fair white flying clouds at 9 in the morning" of a July day, or wheelbarrows heaped up with small black cherries on an August afternoon. He bought twenty walnuts for a penny on the 8th of September, and enjoyed a fine perdrigon-plum upon the 4th.

Meanwhile he is working every day at the Museum, feasting upon literary plums and walnuts, searching the original Ledger-Book of the Signet, copying Sir Thomas Wyatt's *Defence* and his poems, discovering "several odd things unknown to our historians," and nursing his old favourite project of a *History of English Poetry*. He spent as a rule four hours a day in the reading-room, this being as much as his very delicate health could bear, for repeated attacks of the gout had made even this amount of motion and cramped repose sometimes very difficult.

On the 23rd of September, 1759, poor Lady Cobham, justly believing herself to be dying, summoned Gray down to Stoke House. She was suffering from dropsy, and being in a very depressed condition of mind, desired him not to leave her. He accordingly remained with her three weeks, and then accompained her and Miss Speed to town, whither Lady Cobham was recommended to come for advice. She still did not wish to part from him, and he stayed until late in November in her house in Hanover Square. He has some picturesque notes of the beautiful old garden at Stoke that autumn, rich with carnations, marygolds and asters, and with great clusters of white grapes on warm south walls. After watching beside Lady Cobham for some weeks, and finding no reason to anticipate a sudden change in her condition, he returned to his own lodging in Southampton Row, and plunged again into MSS. of Lydgate and Hoccleve.

It was while Gray was quietly vegetating in Bloomsbury that an event occurred of which he was quite unconscious, which yet has singularly endeared him to the memory of Englishmen. On the evening of the 12th of September, 1759,—while Gray, sauntering back from the British Museum to his lodgings, noted that the weather was cloudy, with a S.S.W. wind,—on the other side of the Atlantic the English forces lay along the river Montmorency, and looked anxiously across at Quebec and at the fateful heights of Abraham. When night-fall came.

and before the gallant four thousand obeyed the word of command to steal across the river, General Wolfe, the young officer of thirty-three, who was next day to win death and immortality in victory, crept along in a boat from post to post to see that all was ready for the expedition. It was a fine, silent evening, and as they pulled along, with muffled oars, the General recited to one of his officers who sat with him in the stern of the boat nearly the whole of Gray's *Elegy in a Country Churchyard*, adding, as he concluded, "I would prefer being the author of that Poem to the glory of beating the French to-morrow." Perhaps no finer compliment was ever paid by the man of action to the man of imagination, and, sanctified, as it were, by the dying lips of the great English hero, the poem seems to be raised far above its intrinsic rank in literature, and to demand our respect as one of the acknowledged glories of our race and language. This beautiful anecdote of Wolfe rests on the authority of Professor Robison, the mathematician, who was a recruit in the engineers during the attack upon Quebec, and happened to be present in the boat when the General recited Gray's poem.

Poor Gray, ever pursued by the terrors of arson, had a great fright in the last days of November in this year. A fire broke out in the house of an organist on the opposite side of Southampton Row, and the poor householder was burned to death; the fire spread to the house of Gray's lawyer, who fortunately saved his papers. A few nights later, the poet was roused by a conflagration close at hand in Lincoln's Inn Fields. "'Tis strange," he says, in a spirit of desperation, "that we all of us here in town lay ourselves down every night on our funereal pile, ready made, and compose ourselves to rest, while every drunken footman and drowsy old woman has a candle

L

ready to light it before the morning." It is rather difficult to know what, even in so pastoral a Bloomsbury,
Gray did with a sow, for which he thanks Wharton heartily
in April 1760.

In the spring of this year Gray first met Sterne, who
had just made an overwhelming success with *Tristram
Shandy*, and who was sitting to Sir Joshua Reynolds.
Gray's opinion of Sterne was not entirely unfavourable ;
the great humorist was polite to him, and his works were
not by nature so perplexing to Gray as those of Smollett
and Fielding. The poet was interested in Sterne's newly-
discovered emotion, sensibility, and told Nicholls afterwards that in this sort of pathos Sterne never failed ; for
his wit he had less patience, and frankly disapproved
his tittering insinuations. He said that there was good
writing and good sense in Sterne's *Sermons*, and spoke of
him, when he died in 1768, with some respect. A less
famous but pleasanter man, whose acquaintance Gray
began to cultivate about this time was Benjamin Stilling-
fleet, the Blue Stocking.

In April 1760 Lady Cobham was at last released
from her sufferings. She left the whole of her property, 30,000*l*., to Harriet Speed, besides the house in
Hanover Square, plate, jewels, and much blue and white
china. Gray tells Wharton darkly that Miss Speed
does not know her own mind, but that he knows his.
The movements of this odd couple during the summer
of 1760 are very dim to us and perplexing. Why they
seem associated in some sort of distant intimacy from
April to June, why in the latter month they go down together to stay with General Conway and Lady Ailesbury
at Park Place, near Henley, and why Lady Carlisle is of
the party, these are questions that now can only tantalize

us. Gray himself confesses that all the world expected
him to marry Miss Speed, and was astonished that Lady
Cobham only left him 20l. for a mourning ring. It seems
likely on the whole that had he been inclined to endow
Harriet Speed with his gout, his poverty, his melancholy,
and his fitful genius, she would have accepted the respon-
sibility. When she did marry, it was not for money or
position. He probably, for his part, did not feel so pas-
sionately inclined to her as to convince himself that he
ought to think of marriage. He put an air of Geminiani
to words for her, not very successfully, and he wrote one
solitary strain of amatory experience :—

> With beauty, with pleasure surrounded, to languish,
> To weep without knowing the cause of my anguish,
> To start from short slumbers, and wish for the morning—
> To close my dull eyes when I see it returning,
> Sighs sudden and frequent, looks ever dejected,—
> Words that steal from my tongue, by no meaning connected!
> Ah! say, fellow-swains, how these symptoms befell me?
> They smile, but reply not—Sure Delia will tell me!

For a month in the summer of 1760 he lived at Park
Place in the company of Miss Speed, Lady Ailesbury, and
Lady Carlisle, who laughed from morning to night, and
would not allow him to give way to what they called his
"sulkiness." They found him a difficult guest to entertain.
Lady Ailesbury told Walpole afterwards that one day when
they went out for a picnic, Gray only opened his lips once,
and then merely to say, "Yes, my Lady, I believe so."
His own account shows that his nerves were in a very
weary condition. "Company and cards at home, parties
by land and water abroad, and what they call *doing something*, that is, racketing about from morning to night, are
occupations, I find, that wear out my spirits, especially in

a situation where one might sit still, and be alone with
pleasure." Early in August he escaped to the quietness
of Cambridge in the Long Vacation, and after this saw
little of Miss Speed. Next January she married a poor
man ten years younger than herself, a Baron de la Peyrière,
and went to live at Viry, on the Lake of Geneva. Here,
long after the death of the poet, she received a Mr. Leman,
and gave into his hands the lines which Gray had addressed to her. So ended his one feeble and shadowy
romance. Gray was not destined to come within the
genial glow of any woman's devotion, except his mother's.
He lived a life apart from the absorbing emotions of
humanity, desirous to sympathize with but not to partake
in the stationary affections and household pleasures of the
race. In the annals of friendship he is eminent; he did
not choose to tempt fortune by becoming a husband and a
father. There are some beautiful words of Sir Thomas
Browne that come before the mind as singularly appropriate
to Gray:—" I never yet cast a true affection on a woman ;
but I have loved my friend, as I do virtue, my soul, my
God."

In July 1760 there were published anonymously *Two
Odes*, addressed to Obscurity and to Oblivion, which were
attacks on Gray and on Mason respectively. It was not
at first recognized that this was a salute fired off by that
group of young satirists from Westminster, of whom Cowper, Lloyd and Churchill are now the best known. These
odes, indeed, were probably a joint production, but the
credit of them was taken by George Colman (the elder)
and by Robert Lloyd, gay young wits of twenty-seven.
The mock odes, in which the manners of Gray and Mason
were fairly well parodied, attracted a good deal more
notice than they were worth, and the *Monthly Review*

challenged the poets to reply. But Gray warned Mason
not to do so. Colman was a friend of Garrick, while
Lloyd was an impassioned admirer of Gray himself, and
there was no venom in the verses. Lloyd, indeed, had
the naïveté to reprint these odes some years afterwards,
in a volume which bore his name, and which contained a
Latin version of the *Elegy in a Country Churchyard*.
Lloyd was a figure of no importance, a mere shadow cast
before by Churchill.

In 1760 Gray became deeply interested in the Erse
Fragments of Macpherson, soon to come before the world
as the epic of *Ossian*. He corresponded with the young
Scotchman of twenty-two, whom he found stupid and ill-
educated, and, in Gray's opinion, quite incapable of having
invented what he was at this time producing. The
elaborate pieces, the narratives of *Croma*, *Fingal* and the
rest, were not at this time thought of, and it seems on the
whole that the romantic fragments so much admired by the
best judges of poetry were genuine. What is interesting
to us in Gray's connexion with Ossian is partly critical and
partly personal. Critically it is very important to see that
the romantic tendency of his mind asserted itself at once
in the presence of this savage poetry. He quotes certain
phrases with high approbation. Ossian says of the
winds, "Their songs are of other worlds:" Gray ex-
claims, "Did you never observe that pause, as the gust
is recollecting itself, and rising upon the ear in a shrill and
plaintive note like the swell of an Æolian harp? I do
assure you there is nothing in the world so like the voice
of a spirit." These pieces produced on him just the same
effect of exciting and stimulating mystery that had been
caused by his meeting with the ballads of *Gil Morice* and
Chevy Chase in 1757. He began to feel, just as the power

of writing verse was leaving him or seemed to be declining,
that the deepest chords of his nature as a poet had never
yet been struck.   From this time forth what little serious
poetry he wrote was distinctly romantic, and his studies
were all in the direction of what was savage and archaic,
the poetry of the precursors of our literature in England
and Scotland, the runic chants of the Scandinavians, the
war-songs of the primitive Gaels, everything, in fact, which
for a century past had been looked upon as ungenteel and
incorrect in literature.   Personally what is interesting in
his introduction to Ossian is his sudden sympathy with
men like Adam Smith and David Hume, for whom he
had been trained in the school of Warburton and Hurd to
cultivate a fanatic hatred.   In the summer of 1760 a
variety of civilities on the absorbing question of the Erse
Fragments passed between him and the great historian.
Hume had written to a friend:—"It gives me pleasure to
find that a person of so fine a taste as Mr. Gray approves of
these fragments, as it may convince us that our fondness
of them is not altogether founded on national preposses-
sion," and Gray was encouraged by this to enter into
correspondence of a most friendly kind with the dangerous
enemy of orthodoxy.   He never quite satisfied himself
about Ossian; his last word on that subject is:—"For
me, I admire nothing but *Fingal*, yet I remain still in
doubt about the authenticity of these poems, though in-
clining rather to believe them genuine in spite of the world.
Whether they are the inventions of antiquity, or of a
modern Scotchman, either case to me is alike unaccount-
able.   Je m'y perds."   Modern scholarship has really not
progressed much nearer to a solution of the puzzle.

Partly at the instance of Mason, Gray took a considerable interest in the exhibition of the Society of Arts at the

Adelphi, in 1760. This was the first collection of the kind made in London, and was the nucleus out of which the institution of the Royal Academy sprang. The genius of this first exhibition was Paul Sandby, a man whom Mason thought he had discovered, and whom he was constantly recommending to Gray. Sandby, afterwards eminent as the first great English water-colour painter, had at this time hardly discovered his vocation, though he was in his thirty-fifth year. He was still designing architecture and making profitless gibes and lampoons against Hogarth. Gray and Mason appear to have drawn his attention to landscape of a romantic order, and in October, 1760, Gray tells Wharton of a great picture in oils, illustrating *The Bard*, with Edward I. in the foreground and Snowdon behind, which Sandby and Mason have concocted together, and which is to be the former's exhibition picture for 1761. Sandby either repeated this subject, or took another from the same poem, for there exists a picture of his, without any Edward I., in which the Bard is represented as plunging into the roaring tide, with his lyre in his hand, and Snowdon behind him.

During the winter of 1760 and the spring of 1761 Gray seems to have given his main attention to early English poetry. He worked at the British Museum with indefatigable zeal, copying with his own hand the whole of the very rare 1579 edition of Gawin Douglas' *Palace of Honour*, which he greatly admired, and composing those interesting and learned studies on *Metre* and on the *Poetry of John Lydgate* which Mathias first printed in 1814.

Warburton had placed in his hands a rough sketch which Pope had drawn out of a classification of the British Poets. Pope's knowledge did not go very far, and Gray seems to have first formed the notion of himself writing a

History of English Poetry while correcting his predecessor's errors. The scheme of his history is one which will
probably be followed by the historian of our poetry, when
such a man arises; Gray proposed to open by a full
examination of the Provençal school, in which he saw
the germ of all the modern poetry of Western Europe;
from Provence to France and Italy, and thence to England
the transition was to be easy; and it was only after bringing up the reader to the mature style of Gower and Chaucer,
that a return was to be made to the native, that is the
Anglo-Saxon elements of our literature. Gray made a
variety of purchases for use in this projected compila-
tion, and according to his MS. account-book he had
some "finds" which are enough to make the modern
bibliomaniac mad with envy. He gave sixpence each for
the 1587 edition of Golding's *Ovid* and the 1607 edition
of Phaer's *Æneid*, while the 1550 edition of John
Heywood's *Fables* seems to have been thrown in for
nothing, to make up the parcel. Needless to say that
after consuming months and years in preparing materials for his great work, Gray never completed or even
began it, and in April, 1770, learning from Hurd that
Thomas Warton was about to essay the same labour, he
placed all his notes and memoranda in Warton's hands.
The result, which Gray never lived to see, was creditable
and valuable, and even now is not entirely antiquated; it
was very different, however, from what the world would
have had every right to expect from Gray's learning, taste
and method.

Two short poems composed in the course of 1761 next
demand our attention. The first is a sketch of Gray's
own character, which was found in one of his note-
books :—

Too poor for a bribe, and too proud to importune,
He had not the method of making a fortune;
Could love, and could hate, so was thought somewhat odd;
No very great wit, he believed in a God;
A post or a pension he did not desire,
But left church and state to Charles Townshend and Squire.

It has been commonly supposed that these lines suggested to Goldsmith his character of Burke in *Retaliation*. Charles Townshend is the famous statesman, surnamed the Weathercock; the Rev. Samuel Squire was much more obscure, an intriguing fellow of a Cambridge college who had just contrived to wriggle into the bishopric of St. David's. Warburton said that Squire "made religion his trade." At the storming of Belleisle, June, 13, 1761, Sir William Williams, a young soldier with whom Gray was slightly aquainted, was killed, and the Montagus, who proposed to erect a monument to him, applied to Gray for an epitaph. After considerable difficulty, in August of that year, Gray contrived to squeeze out three of his stately quatrains. Walpole describes Williams as "a gallant and ambitious young man, who had devoted himself to war and politics," and to whom Frederic Montagu was warmly attached. Gray, however, expresses no strong personal feeling, and did not indeed know much of the subject of his elegy. It is curious that in a letter to Dr. Brown, dated Oct. 23, 1760, Gray mentions that Sir W. Williams is starting on the expedition that proved fatal to him, and predicts that he "may lay his fine Vandyck head in the dust."

For two years Gray had kept his rooms at Cambridge locked up, except during the Long Vacation, but in the early spring of 1761, he began to think of returning to what was really home for him. He ran down for a few

days in January, but found Cambridge too cold, and told
Dr. Brown not to expect him till the codlin hedge at
Pembroke was out in blossom.   Business, however, delayed
him, against his will, until June, when he settled in
college.   In September he came up again to London to be
present at the Coronation of George III., on which occasion he was accommodated with a place in the Lord Chamberlain's box.   "The Bishop of Rochester would have
dropped the crown if it had not been pinned to the cushion,
and the king was often obliged to call out, and set matters
right; but the sword of state had been entirely forgot, so
Lord Huntingdon was forced to carry the lord mayor's
great two-handed sword instead of it.   This made it later
than ordinary before they got under their canopies and set
forward.   I should have told you that the old Bishop of
Lincoln, with his stick, went doddling by the side of the
Queen, and the Bishop of Chester had the pleasure of
bearing the gold paten.   When they were gone, we went
down to dinner, for there were three rooms below, where
the Duke of Devonshire was so good as to feed us with
great cold sirloins of beef, legs of mutton, fillets of veal, and
other substantial viands and liquors, which we devoured all
higgledy-piggledy, like porters ; after which every one
scrambled up again, and seated themselves."

In the winter of 1761 Gray was curiously excited by
the arrival at Cambridge of Mr. Delaval, a former fellow
of the college, bringing with him a set of musical glasses.
To Mason, Gray writes on the 8th of December :—

Of all loves come to Cambridge out of hand, for here is Mr.
Delaval and a charming set of glasses that sing like nightingales; and we have concerts every other night, and shall stay
here this month or two; and a vast deal of good company, and
a whale in pickle just come from Ipswich ; and the man will

not die, and Mr. Wood is gone to Chatsworth; and there is nobody but you and Tom and the curled dog, and do not talk of
the charge, for we will make a subscription; besides, we know
you always come when you have a mind.

As early as 1760, probably during one of his flying visits
to Cambridge, Gray had a young fellow introduced to him
of whom he seems at that time to have taken no notice,
but who was to become the most intimate and valued of
his friends.   No person has left so clear and circum-
stantial an account of the appearance, conduct, and sayings
of Gray as the Rev. Norton Nicholls of Blundeston, in
1760 an undergraduate at Trinity Hall, and between
eighteen and nineteen years of age.   Nicholls afterwards
told Mathias that the lightning brightness of Gray's eye
was what struck him most in his first impression, and he
used the phrase "*folgorante sguardo*" to express what
he meant.   A little later than this, at a social gathering
in the rooms of a Mr. Lobbs, at Peterhouse, Nicholls
formed one of a party who collected round Gray's chair
and listened to his bright conversation.   The young man
was too modest to join in the talk, until, in reply to something that had been said on the use of bold metaphors in
poetry, Gray quoted Milton's " The sun to me is dark, and
silent as the moon;" upon this Nicholls ventured to ask
whether this might not possibly be imitated from Dante, "Mi
ripingeva la dove il sol tace."   Gray turned quickly round
and said, " Sir, do you read Dante?" and immediately
entered into conversation with him.   He found Nicholls
an intelligent and sympathetic student of literature; he
chiefly addressed him through the remainder of the evening;
and when they came to part, he pressed him to visit him
in his own rooms at Pembroke.

Gray had never forgotten the Italian which he had learned in his youth, and he was deeply read in Dante, Petrarch, Ariosto, and Tasso, while disdaining those popular poets of the eighteenth century who at that time enjoyed more consideration in their native land than the great classics of the country.   One of his proofs of favour to his young friend Nicholls was to lend him his marked and annotated copy of Petrarch ; and he was pleased when Nicholls was the first to trace in the *Purgatorio* the lines which suggested a phrase in the *Elegy in a Country Churchyard*.   It was doubtless with a side-glance at his own starved condition of genius that he told Nicholls that he thought it "an advantage to Dante to have been produced in a rude age of strong and uncontrolled passions, when the Muse was not checked by refinement and the fear of criticism."   For the next three years we must consider Gray as constantly cheered by the sympathy and enthusiasm of young Nicholls, though it is not until 1764 that we come upon the first of the invaluable letters which the latter received from his great friend.

Nothing could be more humdrum than Gray's existence about this time.   There is no sign of literary life in him, and the whole year 1762 seems only broken by a journey northwards in the summer.   Towards the end of June, he went to stay at York for a fortnight with Mason, whose "insatiable avarice," as Gray calls it in writing to him, had been lulled for a little while by the office of residentiary of York Cathedral.   Mason was now grown lazy and gross, sitting "like a Japanese divinity, with his hands folded on his fat belly," and so prosperous that Gray recommends him to "shut his insatiable repining mouth." There was a fund of good-humour about Mason, and under all the satire of his friend he does not seem to have shown

the least irritation.   From York, Gray went on to Durham,
to stay with Wharton at Old Park, where he was extremely
happy ; "we take in no newspaper or magazine, but the
cream and butter are beyond compare."   He made a long
stay, and rather late in the autumn set out for a tour in
Yorkshire by himself.   Through driving rain he saw what
he could of Richmond and of Ripon, but was fortunate enough
to secure some gleams of sunshine for an examination of
Fountains Abbey.   At Sheffield, then pastoral and pretty
still, he admired the charming situation of the town, and
so came at last to Chatsworth and Hardwicke, at which
latter place "one would think Mary Queen of Scots was
but just walked down into the park with her guard for
half an hour."   After passing through Chesterfield and
Mansfield, Gray descended the Trent, spent two or three
days at Nottingham, and came up to London by the coach.

He arrived to find letters awaiting him, and a great
pother.   Dr. Shallet Turner of Peterhouse, Professor of
Modern History and Modern Languages at Cambridge, had
been dead a fortnight, and Gray's friends were very anxious
to secure the vacant post for him.   The chair had been
founded by George I. in 1724, and the stipend was 400*l.*
It was not expected that any lectures should be given; as
a matter of fact not one lecture was delivered until after
Gray's death.   Shallet Turner had succeeded Samuel
Harris, the first professor, in 1735, and had held the sinecure for twenty-seven years.   Gray's friends encouraged
him to think that Lord Bute would look favourably on his
claims, partly because of his fame as a poet, and partly
because Bute's creature, Sir Henry Erskine, was a great
friend of Gray's; but Sir Francis Blake Delaval had in
the meantime secured the interest of the Duke of Newcastle for his own kinsman.   Early in November it was

generally reported that Delaval had been appointed, but a
month later the post was actually given to Lawrence
Brockett of Trinity, who held it until 1768, when he was
succeeded by Gray.   This is the only occasion upon which
the poet, in an age when the most greedy and open demands
for promotion were considered in no way dishonourable,
persuaded his haughty and independent spirit to ask for anything; in this one case he gave way to the importunities of a
crowd of friends, who declared that he had but to put out
his hand and take the fruit that was ready to drop into it.

In the spring of 1763 Gray was recalled to the pursuit
of literature by the chance that a friend of his, a Mr.
Howe, of Pembroke, while travelling in Italy, met the
celebrated critic and commentator Count Francesco Algarotti, to whom he presented Gray's poems.   The Count
read them with rapturous admiration, and passed them on
to the young poet Agostino Paradisi, with a recommendation that he should translate them into Italian.   The
reputation of Algarotti was then a European one, and Gray
was very much flattered at the graceful and ardent compliments of so famous a connoisseur.   "I was not born so
far from the sun," he says, in a letter dated February 17th,
1763, "as to be ignorant of Count Algarotti's name and
reputation; nor am I so far advanced in years, or in philosophy, as not to feel the warmth of his approbation.   The
odes in question, as their motto shows, were meant to be
vocal to the intelligent alone.   How few *they* were in my
own country, Mr. Howe can testify; and yet my ambition
was terminated by that small circle.   I have good reason to
be proud, if my voice has reached the ear and apprehension
of a stranger, distinguished as one of the best judges in
Europe."   Algarotti replied that England, which had
already enjoyed a Homer, an Archimedes, a Demosthenes,

now possessed a Pindar also, and enclosed "observations, that is panegyrics" on the *Odes*. For some months the correspondence of Count Algarotti enlivened "the nothing-ness" of Gray's history at Cambridge, "a place," he says, "where no events grow, though we preserve those of former days by way of *hortus siccus* in our libraries." In Novem-ber 1763 the Count announced his intention of visiting England, where he proposed to publish a magnificent edition of his own works; Gray seems to have anticipated pleasure from his company, but Algarotti never came, and soon died rather unexpectedly, in Italy, on the 24th of May, 1764, at the age of fifty-two.

We possess some of the notes which Gray took of the habits of flowers and birds, thus anticipating the charming observations of Gilbert White. At Cam-bridge, in 1763, crocus and hepatica were blossoming through the snow in the college garden on the 12th of February; nine days later brought the first white butter-fly; on the 5th of March Gray heard the thrush sing, and on the 8th the skylark. The same warm day which brought the lark opened the blossom-buds of the apricots, and the almond-trees for once found themselves out-run in the race of spring. These notes show the quickness of Gray's eye, and his quiet ways. It is only the silent, clear-sighted man that knows on what day the first fall of lady-birds is seen, or observes the redstart sitting on her eggs. Gray's notes for the spring of 1763 read like fragments of a beautiful poem, and are scarcely less articulate than that little trill of improvised song which Norton Nicholls has preserved:—

> There pipes the wood-lark, and the song-thrush there
> Scatters his loose notes in the waste of air,

a couplet which Gray made one spring morning, as Nicholls

and he were walking in the fields in the neighbourhood of Cambridge.

To this period should be attributed the one section of Gray's poems which it is impossible to date with exactness, namely the romantic lyrics paraphrased, in short measures, from Icelandic and Gaelic sources.[1] When these pieces were published, in 1768, Gray prefixed to them an "advertisement," which was not reprinted. In this he connected them with his projected *History of English Poetry*; "in the introduction" to that work, "he meant to have produced some specimens of the style that reigned in ancient times among the neighbouring nations, or those who had subdued the greater part of this island, and were only progenitors : the following three imitations made a part of them." The three imitations are *The Fatal Sisters*, *The Descent of Odin*, and *The Triumphs of Owen*. To these must be added the smaller fragments, *The Death of Hoel*, *Caradoc*, and *Conon*, discovered among Gray's papers, and first printed by Mason. These, then, form a division of Gray's poetical work not inconsiderable in extent, remarkably homogeneous in style and substance, and entirely distinct from anything else which he wrote. In these paraphrases of archaic chants he appears as a purely romantic poet, and heralds the approach of Sir Walter Scott, and the whole revival of northern romance. The Norse pieces are perhaps more interesting than the Celtic ; they are longer, and to modern scholarship seem more authentic, at all events more in the general current of literature. Moreover they were translated direct from the Icelandic, whereas there is no absolute proof that Gray was a Welsh scholar. It may well inspire us with admiration of the poet's intellectual

[1] I notice that the *The Fatal Sisters* and *The Descent of Odin* bear the date 1761 in the Pembroke MSS.

energy to find that he had mastered a language which was
hardly known, at that time, by any one in Europe, except
a few learned Icelanders, whose native tongue made it
easy for them to understand Norrœna.   Gray must have
puzzled it out for himself, probably with the help of the
Index Linguæ Scytho-Scandicae of Verelius.   At that
time what he rightly calls the Norse Tongue was looked
upon as a sort of mystery ; it was called " Runick," and its
roots were supposed to be derived from the Hebrew.   The
Fatal Sisters is a lay of the eleventh century, the text of
which Gray found in one of the compilations of Torfœus
(Thormod Torveson), a great collector of ancient Icelandic
vellums at the close of the seventeenth century.   It is a
monologue, sung by one of the Valkyriur or Choosers of
the Slain to her three sisters ; the measure is one of great
force and fire, an alternate rhyming of seven-syllable
lines, of which this is a specimen :—

> Now the storm begins to lower,
>   (Haste, the loom of Hell prepare !)
> Iron-sleet of arrowy shower
>   Hurtles in the darkened air.
>
>   .   .   .   .
>
> Ere the ruddy sun be set
>   Pikes must shiver, javelins sing,
> Blade with clattering buckler meet,
>   Hauberk crash, and helmet ring.
>
>   .   .   .   .
>
> Sisters, hence with spurs of speed ;
>   Each her thundering faulchion wield ;
> Each bestride her sable steed,
>   Hurry, hurry to the field !

The *Descent of Odin* is a finer poem, better paraphrased.
Gray found the original in a book by Bartolinus, one of the

M

five great physicians of that name who flourished in Denmark during the seventeenth century.   The poem itself is
the *Vegtamskvida*, one of the most powerful and mysterious
of those ancient lays which form the earliest collection
we possess of Scandinavian poetry.   It is probable that
Gray never saw the tolerably complete but very inaccurate
edition of *Sœmundar Edda* which existed in his time, nor
knew the wonderful history of this collection, which was
discovered in Iceland, in 1643, by Brynjólfr Sveinnson,
Bishop of Skálaholt.   The text which Gray found in
Bartolinus, however, was sufficiently true to enable him
to make a better translation of the *Vegtamskvida* than
any which has been attempted since, and to make us
deeply regret that he did not " imitate " more of these
noble Eddaic chants.   He even attempts a philological
ingenuity, for, finding that Odin, to conceal his true nature
from the Völva, calls himself Vegtam, Gray translates this
strange word " traveller," evidently tracing it to *veg*, a
way.   He omits the first stave, which recounts how the
Æsir sat in council to deliberate on the dreams of Balder,
and he also omits four spurious stanzas, in this showing a
critical tact little short of miraculous, considering the condition of scholarship at that time.   The version itself is as
poetical as it is exact :—

> Right against the eastern gate,
> By the moss-grown pile he sate;
> Where long of yore to sleep was laid
> The dust of the prophetic Maid.
> Facing to the northern clime,
> Thrice he traced the runic rhyme;
> Thrice pronounced, in accents dread,
> The thrilling verse that wakes the Dead;
> Till from out the hollow ground
> Slowly breathed a sullen sound.

or,

> Mantling in the goblet see
> The pure beverage of the bee,
> O'er it hangs the shield of gold;
> 'Tis the drink of Balder bold.
> Balder's head to death is given.
> Pain can reach the sons of Heaven!
> Unwilling I my lips unclose,
> Leave me, leave me, to repose,

must be compared with the original to show how thoroughly the terse and rapid evolution of the strange old lay has been preserved, though the concise expression has throughout been modernized and rendered intelligible.

In these short pieces we see the beginning of that return to old Norse themes which has been carried so far and so brilliantly by later poets. It is a very curious thing that Gray in this anticipated, not merely his own countrymen, but the Scandinavians themselves. The first poems in which a Danish poet showed any intelligent appreciation of his national mythology and history, were the *Rolf Krake* and *Balder's Död* of Johannes Ewald, published respectively in 1770 and 1773. Gray therefore takes the precedence not only of Sir Walter Scott, Mr. Morris and other British poets, but even of the countless Danish, Swedish, and German writers who for a century past have celebrated the adventures of the archaic heroes of their race.

In a century which was inclined to begin the history of English poetry with the Life of Cowley, and which distrusted all that was ancient, as being certainly rude and probably worthless, Gray held the opinion, which he expresses in a letter of the 17th of February, 1763, " that without any respect of climates, imagination reigns

in all nascent societies of men, where the necessaries of
life force every one to think and act much for himself."
This critical temper attracted him to the *Edda*, made him
indulgent to Ossian, and led him to see more poetry in the
ancient songs of Wales than most non-Celtic readers can
discover there.   In 1764 Evans published his *Specimens
of Welsh Poetry*, and in that bulky quarto Gray met with
a Latin prose translation of the chant written about 1158
by Gwalchmai, in praise of his master Owen Gwynedd.
The same Evans gave a variety of extracts from the
Welsh epic, the *Gododin*, and three of these fragments
Gray turned into English rhyme.   One has something of
the concision of an epigram from the Greek mythology :—

> Have ye seen the tusky boar,
> Or the bull, with sullen roar,
> On surrounding foes advance ?
> So Caradoc bore his lance.

The others are not nearly equal in poetical merit to the
Scandinavian paraphrases.   Gray does not seem to have
shown these romances to his friends, with the same readi-
ness that he displayed on other occasions.   From critics
like Hurd and Warburton he could expect no approval of
themes taken from an antique civilization.   Walpole, who
did not see these poems till they were printed, asks :—
" Who can care through what horrors a Runic savage
arrived at all the joys and glories they could conceive,—
the supreme felicity of boozing ale out of the skull of an
enemy in Odin's Hall ?"   This is quite a characteristic
expression of that wonderful eighteenth century through
which poor Gray wandered in a life-long exile.   The
author of the *Vegtamskvida* a " Runic savage " !   No
wonder Gray kept his " Imitations " safely out of the
sight of such critics.

CHAPTER VIII.

THE seven remaining years of Gray's life were even less eventful than those which we have already examined. In November 1763 he began to find that a complaint, which had long troubled him, the result of failing constitution, had become almost constant. For eight or nine months he was an acute sufferer, until in July 1764 he consented to undergo the operation without which he could not have continued to live. Dr. Wharton volunteered to come up from Durham, and, if not to perform the act, to support his friend in "the perilous hour." But Gray preferred that the Cambridge surgeon should attend him, and the operation was not only performed successfully, but the poet was able to sustain the much-dreaded suffering with fortitude. As he was beginning to get about again, the gout came in one foot, "but so tame you might have stroked it, such a minikin you might have played with it ; in three or four days it had disappeared." This gout which troubled him so constantly, and was fatal to him at last, was hereditary, and not caused by any excess in eating or drinking ; Gray was, in fact, singularly abstemious, and it was one of the accusations of his enemies that he affected to be so dainty that he could touch nothing less delicate than apricot marmalade.

While Gray was lying ill, Lord Chancellor Hardwicke died, at the age of seventy-four, on the 16th of May 1764. The office of Seneschal of the University was thus vacated, and there ensued a very violent contest, the result of which was that Philip Hardwicke succeeded to his father's honours by a majority of one, and the other candidate, the notorious John, Earl of Sandwich, though supported by the aged Dr. Roger Long and other clerical magnates, was rejected. Gray, to whom the tarnished reputation of Lord Sandwich was in the highest degree abhorrent, swelled the storm of electioneering by a lampoon, *The Candidate*, beginning :—

> When sly Jemmy Twitcher had smugged up his face,
> With a lick of court white-wash, and pious grimace,
> A-wooing he went, where three sisters of old
> In harmless society guttle and scold.

Lord Sandwich found that this squib was not without its instant and practical effect, and he attempted to win so dangerous an opponent to his side. What means he adopted cannot be conjectured, but they were unsuccessful. Lord Sandwich said to Cradock, " I have my private reasons for knowing Gray's absolute inveteracy." The *Candidate* found its way into print long after Gray's death, but only in a fragmentary form ; and the same has hitherto been true of *Tophet*, of which I am able to give, for the first time, a complete text from the Pembroke MSS. One of Gray's particular friends, " placid Mr. Tyson of Bene't College," made a drawing of the Rev. Henry Etough, a converted Jew, a man of slanderous and violent temper, who had climbed into high preferment in the Church of England. Underneath this very rude and hideous caricature Gray wrote these lines :—

Thus Tophet look'd : so grinn'd the brawling fiend,
Whilst frighted prelates bow'd and call'd him friend ;
I saw them bow, and, while they wish'd him dead,
With servile simper nod the mitred head.
Our mother-church, with half-averted sight,
Blush'd as she bless'd her griesly proselyte ;
Hosannahs rang through hell's tremendous borders,
And Satan's self had thoughts of taking orders.

These two pieces, however, are very far from being the only effusions of the kind which Gray wrote. Mason appears to have made a collection of Gray's Cambridge squibs, which he did not venture to print. A *Satire upon the Heads, or Never a barrel the better Herring*, a comic piece in which Gray attacked the prominent heads of houses, was printed by me in 1884 from a MS. in possession of the late Lord Houghton. These squibs are said to have been widely circulated in Cambridge, so widely as to frighten the timid poet, and to have been retained as part of the tradition of Pembroke common-room until long after Gray's death. I am told that Mason's set of copies of these poems, of which I have seen a list, turned up, during the present century, in the library of a cathedral in the north of England. This may give some clue to their ultimate discovery ; they might prove to be coarse and slight, they could not fail to be biographically interesting.

In October 1764 Gray set out upon what he called his "Lilliputian travels" in the south of England. He went down by Winchester to Southampton, stayed there some weeks, and then returned to London by Salisbury, Wilton, Amesbury and Stonehenge. " I proceed to tell you," he says to Norton Nicholls, "that my health is much improved by the sea ; not that I drank it, or bathed in it, as the *common people* do. No ! I only walked by

it and looked upon it." His description of Netley Abbey,
in a letter to Dr. Brown, is very delicate :—" It stands in
a little quiet valley, which gradually rises behind the
ruins into a half-circle crowned with thick wood. Before
it, on a descent, is a thicket of oaks, that serves to veil it
from the broad day, and from profane eyes, only leaving a
peep on both sides, where the sea appears glittering
through the shade, and vessels, with their white sails, glide
across and are lost again. . . . I should tell you that the
ferryman who rowed me, a lusty young fellow, told me
that he would not, for all the world, pass a night at the
Abbey, there were such things seen near it." Still more
picturesque, indeed showing an eye for nature which
was then without a precedent in modern literature, is
this passage from a letter of this time to Norton
Nicholls :—

I must not close my letter without giving you one principal
event of my history; which was, that (in the course of my late
tour) I set out one morning before five o'clock, the moon shining
through a dark and misty autumnal air, and got to the sea-
coast time enough to be at the Sun's levée. I saw the clouds
and dark vapours open gradually to right and left, rolling over
one another in great smoky wreaths, and the tide (as it flowed
gently in upon the sands) first whitening, then slightly tinged
with gold and blue; and all at once a little line of insufferable
brightness that (before I can write these few words) was grown
to half an orb, and now to a whole one, too glorious to be distinctly seen. It is very odd it makes no figure on paper; yet
I shall remember it as long as the sun, or at least as long as
I endure. I wonder whether anybody ever saw it before! I
hardly believe it.

In November Gray was laid up again with illness,
being threatened this time with blindness, a calamity

which passed off favourably.   He celebrated the death of Churchill, which occurred at this time, by writing what he calls " The Temple of Tragedy."   We do not know what this may have been, but it would not be inspired by love of Churchill, who, in the course of his brief rush through literature in the guise of a " rogue " elephant, had annoyed Gray, though he had never tossed him or trampled on him.   Gray bought all the pamphlet-satires of Churchill as they appeared, and enriched them with annotations.   In his collection, the *Ghost* alone is missing, perhaps because of the allusions it contained to himself.

On the 24th of December, 1764, that Gothic romance, the *Castle of Otranto*, was published anonymously.   It was almost universally attributed to Gray, to the surprise and indignation of Horace Walpole, who said of his own work, modestly enough, that people must be fools indeed to think such a trifle worthy of a genius like Gray.   The reputation of the poet as an antiquarian and a lover of romantic antiquity probably led to this mistake.   At Cambridge another error prevailed, as Gray announces to Walpole within a week of the publication of the book. " It engages our attention here, makes some of us cry a little, and all in general afraid to go to bed o' nights. We take it for a translation, and should believe it to be a true story if it were not for St. Nicholas."   This novel, poor as it is, was a not inconsiderable link in the chain of romantic revival started by Gray.

We have little record of the poet's life during the early months of 1765.   In June he was laid up with gout at York, while paying a visit to Mason, and in July went on to drink the waters and walk by the sea at Hartlepool. From this place he sent to Mason some excellent stanzas which have never found their way into his works ; they

are supposed to be indited by William Shakespeare in
person, and to be a complaint of his sufferings at the hands
of his commentators. The poem is in the metre of the
Elegy, and is a very grave specimen of the mock-heroic
style :—

> Better to bottom tarts and cheesecakes nice,
>   Better the roast meat from the fire to save,
> Better be twisted into caps for spice,
>   Than thus be patched and cobbled in one's grave.

What would Gray, and still more what would Shakespeare say to the vapid confusion of opinions which have
been laid on the bard's memory during the century that
now intervenes between these verses and ourselves ;—
a heap of dirt and stones which he must laboriously
shovel away who would read the true inscription on the
Prophet's tomb? For criticism of the type which has
now become so common, for the counting of syllables and
weighing of commas, Gray, with all his punctilio and his
minute scholarship, had nothing but contempt : —

> Much I have borne from cankered critic's spite,
>   From fumbling baronets, and poets small,
> Pert barristers, and parsons nothing bright:—
>   But what awaits me now is worst of all.

Mason at last, at the age of forty, had fallen in love
with a lady of small fortune and less personal appearance,
but very sweet manners ; and while Gray was still lingering
in the North his friend married. Meantime Gray passed
on to Old Park, and spent the month of August with the
Whartons. From this place he went to stay with Lord
Strathmore at Hetton, in Durham, and towards the beginning of September set out with his host and Major Lyon,

his brother, for Scotland. The first night was passed at
Tweedmouth, and the second at Edinburgh ("that most picturesque at a distance, and nastiest when near, of all capital
cities "). Gray was instantly received with honour by the
Scotch literati. On the evening of his arrival he supped
with Dr. W. Robertson and other leading men of letters.
Next day the party crossed the Forth in Lord Strathmore's yawl, and reached Perth, and by dinner-time on the
fourth day arrived at Glamis. Here Gray was extremely
happy for some bright weeks, charmed with the beauty of
the scenery and the novelty of the life, soothed and
delighted by the refined hospitality of the Lyons, three of
whom, including Lord Strathmore, he had known as
undergraduates at Cambridge, and enchanted to hear
spoken and sung on all sides of him the magical language
of Ossian. On the 11th of September Lord Strathmore
took him for a tour of five days in the Highlands, showed
him Dunkeld, Taymouth, and the falls of Tummell, the
Pass of Killiekrankie, Blair-Athol and the peaks of the
Grampians ; " in short," he says, " since I saw the Alps, I
have seen nothing sublime till now."

Immediately on his arrival at Glamis, he had received an
exceedingly polite letter from the poet Beattie, who was a
professor at Aberdeen, pressing him to visit that city, and
requesting, that, if this was impossible, he himself might be
allowed to travel southward to Glamis, to present his compliments to Gray. At the same time the University of
Aberdeen offered him the degree of doctor of laws. Gray
declined both the invitation and the honour, but said that
Lord Strathmore would be very glad to see Beattie at Glamis.
The younger poet accordingly posted to lay his enthusiasm at
the feet of the elder, and Gray received him with unwonted
openness and a sort of intimate candour rare with him.

Beattie reports, among other things, that Dryden was
mentioned by him with scant respect, upon which Gray
remarked "that if there was any excellence in his own
numbers, he had learned it wholly from that great poet.
And pressed him with great earnestness to study him, as
his choice of words and versification were singularly
happy and harmonious."

Gray came back from the mountains with feelings far
other than those in which Dr. Johnson indulged when he
found himself safe once more in the latitude of Fleet
Street. "I am returned from Scotland," says the poet,
"charmed with my expedition ; it is of the Highlands I
speak ; the Lowlands are worth seeing once, but the
mountains are ecstatic, and ought to be visited in pilgrim-
age once a year. None but these monstrous children of
God know how to join so much beauty with so much horror.
A fig for your poets, painters, gardeners and clergymen,
that have not been among them ; their imagination can be
made up of nothing but bowling-greens, flowering shrubs,
horse-ponds, Fleet-ditches, shell-grottoes, and Chinese rails.
Then I had so beautiful an autumn, Italy could hardly
produce a nobler scene, and this so sweetly contrasted with
that perfection of nastiness, and total want of accommo-
dation, that Scotland can only supply."

Mason had married on the 25th of September, and greatly
desired that Gray, when passing southward towards the end
of October, should come and be the witness of his felicity
at Aston, but Gray excused himself on the grounds that
his funds were exhausted, and went straight through to
London. There he found his old friend Harriet Speed,
now Madame de la Peyrière, whose husband was in the
Italian diplomatic service. She was exceedingly glad to
receive him, and welcomed him with two little dogs on

her lap, a cockatoo on her shoulder, a piping bullfinch at her elbow, and a strong suspicion of rouge on her cheeks. For about six months after the tour in Scotland Gray enjoyed very tolerable health, remaining however entirely indolent as far as literature was concerned. When Walpole told him he ought to write more, he replied:—"What has one to do, when turned of fifty, but really to think of finishing? However, I will be candid, for you seem to be so with me, and avow to you, that till fourscore and upwards, whenever the humour takes me, I will write; because I like it, and because I like myself better when I do so. If I do not write much it is because I cannot."

Henceforward the chief events in Gray's life were his summer holidays. In May and June, 1766, he paid a visit to the friend whom he called Reverend Billy, the Rev. William Robinson, younger brother of the famous Mrs. Montagu. This gentleman was rector of Denton, in the county of Kent, a little quiet valley some eight miles to the east of Canterbury and near the sea. Gray took the opportunity of visiting Margate and Ramsgate, which were just beginning to become resorts for holiday folk. It is related that at the latter place the friends went to inspect the new pier, then lately completed. Somebody said, seeing it forlorn and empty, "What did they make this pier for?" whereupon Gray smartly replied, "For me to walk on," and proceeded to claim possession of it, by striding along it. He visited the whole coast of Kent, as far as Hythe, in company with Mr. Robinson. The county charmed him : he wrote to Norton Nicholls :—

The country is all a garden, gay, rich, and fruitful, and from the rainy season had preserved, till I left it, all that emerald verdure, which commonly one only sees for the first fortnight of the spring. In the west part of it from every eminence the eye

catches some long winding reach of the Thames or Medway,
with all their navigation; in the east, the sea breaks in upon
you, and mixes its white transient sails and glittering blue
expanse with the deeper and brighter greens of the woods and
the corn.   This last sentence is so fine, I am quite ashamed;
but, no matter! you must translate it into prose. Palgrave,
if he heard it, would cover his face with his pudding sleeve.

He read the *New Bath Guide*, which had just appeared,
and was tempted to indulge in satire of a different sort,
by the neighbourhood of the Formian villa built by the
late Lord Holland at Kingsgate.   These powerful verses
were found in a drawer at Denton after Gray had
left :—

> Old, and abandoned by each venal friend,
>   Here Holland formed the pious resolution,
> To smuggle a few years and try to mend
>   A broken character and constitution.
>
> On this congenial spot he fixed his choice:
>   Earl Goodwin trembled for his neighbouring sand;
> Here sea-gulls scream, and cormorants rejoice,
>   And mariners, though shipwrecked, dread to land.
>
> Here reign the blustering North and blighting East,
>   No tree is heard to whisper, bird to sing;
> Yet Nature could not furnish out the feast,
>   Art he invokes new horrors still to bring.
>
> Here mouldering fanes and battlements arise,
>   Turrets and arches nodding to their fall,
> Unpeopled monastries delude our eyes,
>   And mimic desolation covers all.
>
> "Ah!" said the sighing peer, "had Bute been true,
>   Nor Mungo's, Rigby's, Bradshaw's friendship vain,
> Far better scenes than these had blest our view,
>   And realized the beauties which we feign:

Purged by the sword, and purified by fire,
   Then had we seen proud London's hated walls;
Owls might have hooted in St. Peter's choir,
   And foxes stunk and littered in St. Paul's.

In November 1766 Mason came to visit Gray in his
lodgings in Jermyn Street and brought his wife, "a
pretty, modest, innocent, interesting figure, looking like
eighteen, though she is near twenty-eight." She was far
gone in consumption, but preserved a muscular strength
and constitutional energy which deceived those who surrounded her. The winter of 1766 tried her endurance
very severely, and she gradually sank. On the 27th of
March, 1767, after a married life of only eighteen months,
she expired in Mason's arms, at Bristol. Gray's correspondence through the three months which preceded her
end displays a constant and lively concern, which reached
its climax in the exquisite letter which he wrote to Mason
the day after her death, before the fatal news had reached
him. In the whole correspondence of a man whose unaffected sympathy was always at the service of his friends,
there is no expression of it more touching than this :—

March 28, 1767.

MY DEAR MASON,—I break in upon you at a moment when
we least of all are permitted to disturb our friends, only to
say that you are daily and hourly present to my thoughts.
If the worst be not yet past, you will neglect and pardon
me; but if the last struggle be over, if the poor object of
your long anxieties be no longer sensible to your kindness or to
her own sufferings, allow me (at least in idea, for what could
I do were I present more than this) to sit by you in silence,
and pity from my heart, not her who is at rest, but you who
lose her. May He who made us, the Master of our pleasures
and our pains, preserve and support you. Adieu! I have
long understood how little you had to hope.

About a month earlier than this, at the very early age
of thirty-six, an old acquaintance and quondam college
friend of Gray's, Frederic Hervey, was presented to the
diocese of Cloyne. This was a startling rise in life to a
ne'er-do-weel of good family, who had not six years
before been begging Mason and Gray to help him, and
who soon after this became, not merely Bishop of Derry,
but Earl of Bristol. Gray saw a good deal of him during
the summer of 1767, and describes how they ate four
raspberry puffs together in that historical pastry-cook's at
the corner of Cranbourne Street, and how jolly Hervey
was at finding himself a bishop. Gray's summer holiday
in 1767 was again spent among the mountains. In June
he went down to Aston to console Mason, and with him
visited Dovedale and the wonders of the Peak ; early in
July Gray set out by York to stay with Wharton at Old
Park, from which in August he sent back to Beattie the
manuscript of *The Minstrel*, which that poet had sent,
requesting him to revise it. Gray gave a great deal of
attention to this rather worthless production, which has
no merit save some smoothness in the use of the Spen-
serian stanza, and which owed all its character to a clever
poem in the same manner, published twenty years earlier,
the *Psyche* of Dr. Gloucester Ridley, a poet whose name,
perhaps, may yet one day find an apologist. Gray, however, never grudged to expend his critical labour to the
advantage of a friend, and pruned the luxuriance of *The
Minstrel* with a serious assiduity.

Meanwhile Lord Strathmore was at hand, marrying himself to a great Durham heiress ; Gray made a trip to Hartlepool in August, and coming back stayed with the newly-
wedded earl and countess at their castle of Gibside, near
Ravensworth. On the 29th of August he and Dr. Wharton

set out in a post-chaise by Newcastle and Hexham for the lakes. On their way to Carlisle they got soaked in the rain, and Wharton was taken so ill with asthma at Keswick, that they returned home to Old Park from Cockermouth after hardly a glimpse of the mountains. In the church at Appleby, the epitaph of Anne, Countess of Dorset, amused Gray by its pomposity, and he improvised the following pleasing variation on it :—

> Now clean, now hideous, mellow now, now gruff,
> She swept, she hiss'd, she ripen'd, and grew rough,
> At Brougham, Pendragon, Appleby and Brough.

Mason buried his wife in the Cathedral of Bristol, and on the tablet which bears her name he inscribed a brief elegy which has outlived all the rest of his works, and is still frequently quoted with praise. It runs thus :—

> Take, holy earth ! all that my soul holds dear:
>   Take that best gift which Heaven so lately gave:
> To Bristol's fount I bore with trembling care
>   Her faded form: she bow'd to taste the wave,
> And died. Does Youth, does Beauty, read the line ?
>   Does sympathetic fear their breasts alarm ?
> Speak, dead Maria ! breathe a strain divine:
>   E'en from the grave thou shalt have power to charm.
> Bid them be chaste, be innocent like thee ;
>   Bid them in Duty's sphere as meekly move ;
> And if so fair, from vanity as free,
>   As firm in friendship, and as fond in love,
> *Tell them, though 'tis an awful thing to die,*
>   *('Twas ev'n to thee) yet the dread path once trod,*
> *Heaven lifts its everlasting portals high,*
>   *And bids the pure in heart behold their God.*

The last four lines have the ring of genuine poetry, and surpass the rest of Mason's productions in verse as gold surpasses dross. It is a very curious thing that he does,

N

in fact, owe his position as a poet to some lines which he
did not write himself. As long as he lived, and for many
years after his death, the secret was kept, but at last
Norton Nicholls confessed that the beautiful quatrain in
italics was entirely composed by Gray.   Nicholls was with
the elder poet at the time when the MS. arrived, and
Gray showed it to him, with Mason's last four lines
erased.   Gray said, " That will never do for an ending ;
I have altered it thus," and thereupon wrote in the stanza
as we now know it.   Nicholls says that Mason's finale was
weak, with a languid repetition of some preceding expressions ; and he took the occasion to criticize the whole
of Mason's poetry as feeble and tame.   " No wonder,"
said Gray, " for Mason never gives himself time to think.
If his epithets do not occur readily, he leaves spaces for
them, and puts them in afterwards.   Mason has read too
little and written too much."   It is well that we should
have this side of the question stated, for Mason loves to
insinuate that Gray thought him a poet of superlative
merit.   There was no love lost between Mason and
Nicholls, and if the younger carefully preserved Gray's
verdict on the poetry of the elder, Mason revenged himself by remarking that it was a good thing for Nicholls
that Gray never discovered that he drank like a fish.   We
are reminded of the wars of Bozzy and Piozzi.

In the spring of 1767 Gray met Dodsley, son of the
great publisher and heir to his business, and was asked
by him to consent to the republication of his poems in a
cheap form.   It was found that Bentley's designs were
worn out, and therefore it was determined to omit all
illustrations, and with them the *Long Story*, which Gray
thought would now be unintelligible.   While this trans-
action was loitering along, as Gray's business was apt to

loiter, Beattie wrote to him, in December 1767, to say that Foulis, an enterprising Glasgow publisher, was anxious to produce the same collection. Dodsley made no objection, and so exactly the same matter was put through two presses at the same time. In neither book had Gray any pecuniary interest. There had been no explanatory notes in the *Odes* of 1757, but in reprinting these poems eleven years later, he added a few " out of spite, because the public did not understand the two odes which I called Pindaric, though the first was not very dark, and the second alluded to a few common facts to be found in any sixpenny history of England, by way of question and answer, for the use of children." He added to what had already appeared in 1753 and 1757, the three short archaic romances, lest, as he said to Horace Walpole, " my *works* should be mistaken for the works of a flea, or a pismire. . . . . With all this I shall be but a shrimp of an author." The book, as a matter of fact, had to be eked out with blank leaves and very wide type to reach the sum of 120 nominal pages. Dodsley's edition was not a beautiful volume, but it was cheap : it appeared in July 1768, and before October of the same year two impressions consisting of 2250 copies, had been sold. Foulis came out with his far more handsome Glasgow edition in September, and this also, though a costly book, of which a very large number of copies had been struck off, was sold out by the summer of 1769, when Foulis made Gray, who refused money, a very handsome present of books. During the last years of his life, then, Gray was not only beyond dispute the greatest living English poet, but recognized as being such by the public itself.

To the riotous living of his great enemy, Lord Sandwich, Gray owed the preferment which raised him above

all fear of poverty, or even of temporary pressure of means
during the last three years of his life. On Sunday, the
24th of July, 1768, Professor Lawrence Brockett, who had
been dining with the earl at Hinchinbroke, in Huntingdon-
shire, while riding back to Cambridge, being very drunk,
fell off his horse and broke his neck. The chair of
Modern Literature and Modern Languages, with its 400*l.*
a year, was one of the most valuable sinecures in the
University. Gray was up in London at the time, but his
cousin Miss Dolly Antrobus, for whom he had obtained
the office of post-mistress at Cambridge, instantly wrote
up to town to tell him. He did not stir in the matter.
With an admirable briskness, five obscure dons immediately put themselves forward as candidates, and so little
did Gray expect to receive the place, that he used his
influence for the only man among them who had any
literature in him, Michael Lort the Hellenist. Gray was
not, however, to be overlooked any longer, and on the
27th he received a letter from that elegant and enlightened
statesman, Augustus, Duke of Grafton, offering the Professorship in terms that were delicately calculated to please
and soothe his pride. He was told that he owed his
nomination to the whole cabinet council, and his success
to the King's particular admiration of his genius; the
Duke would not presume to think that the post could be
of advantage to Gray, but trusted that he might be in-
duced to do so much credit to the University. The poet
accepted at once, on the 28th his warrant was signed, and
on the 29th he was summoned to kiss the King's hand.
These were days in which George III. was still addicted
to polite letters, and Gray's friends were anxious to know
the purport of several very gracious speeches which the
King was observed to make to him; but Gray was coy,

and would not tell; when he was pressed, he said, with great simplicity, that the room was so hot and he himself so embarrassed, that he really did not quite know what it was the King did say.

The charge has often been brought against Gray that he delivered no lectures from his chair at Cambridge. It is, of course, very unfortunate that he did not, but it should be remembered that there was nothing singular in this. Not one of his predecessors, from the date of the institution of the professorship, had delivered a single lecture; Gray, indeed, was succeeded by a man of great energy, John Symonds, who introduced a variety of reforms at Cambridge, and, among others, reformed his own office by lecturing. The terms of the patent recommended the professor to find a deputy in one branch of his duty, and Gray delegated the teaching of foreign languages to a young Italian, Agostino Isola, of literary tastes, who survived long enough to teach Tuscan to Wordsworth. It is said that Gray took the opportunity of reading the Italian poets again with Isola, who afterwards became an editor of Tasso. The granddaughter of Gray's deputy was that Emma Isola who became the adopted child of Charles and Mary Lamb. One is glad to know that Gray behaved with great liberality to Isola and also to the French teacher at the University, René La Butte. It is pleasant to record that the opportunity to follow the natural dictates of his heart in this and other instances, he owed to the loyalty of his old schoolfellow, Stonehewer, who was the secretary of the Duke of Grafton, and who lost no time in suggesting Gray's name to his chief.

Poor Gray, for ever pursued by fears of conflagration, was actually in great danger of being burned alive in January 1768, when a part of Pembroke Hall, including

Mason's chambers, was totally destroyed by fire. Two
Methodists, who had been attending a prayer-meeting in
the town, happened to pass very late at night, and gave
the alarm. Gray was roused between two and three in
the morning by the excellent Stephen Hempstead, with
the remark, "Don't be frighted, Sir, but the college is all
of a fire !" No great harm was done, but Mason had to
be lodged a little lower down the street, opposite Peterhouse. After the event of the professorship, Gray found
himself unable to escape from many public shows in which
he had previously pleaded his obscurity with success.
For instance, in August 1768, the University of Cambridge was honoured by a visit from Christian VII., King
of Denmark, who had married the sister of George III.
To escape from the festivities, Gray went off to Newmarket, but there, as he says, "fell into the jaws of the
King of Denmark," was presented to him by the Vice-
chancellor and the Orator, and was brought back to
Cambridge by them, captive, in a chaise.

The Duke of Grafton succeeded the Duke of Newcastle
as Chancellor of the University of Cambridge in 1768, and
Gray, moved by gratitude, though never by expectation,
made an offer through Stonehewer that he should write an
ode to be performed at the ceremony of installation. He
seems to have made the proposal in the last months of the
year. In April 1769, he says:—"I do not guess what
intelligence Stonehewer gave you about my employments,
but the worst employment I have had has been to write
something for music against the Duke of Grafton comes to
Cambridge. I must comfort myself with the intention,
for I know it will bring abuse enough on me : however, it
is done, and given to the Vice-Chancellor, and there is an
end." Norton Nicholls records that Gray considered the

composition of this *Installation Ode* a sort of task, and set
about it with great reluctance ; " it was long after he first
mentioned it to me before he could prevail with himself
to begin the composition.   One morning, when I went to
him as usual after breakfast, I knocked at his door, which
he threw open, and exclaimed with a loud voice,—

'Hence, avaunt ! 'tis holy ground ! '

I was so astonished, that I almost feared he was out of his
senses ; but this was the beginning of the Ode which he
had just composed."   For three months before the event,
the music professor, J. Randall, of King's, waited on Gray
regularly to set the *Installation Ode* to music.   It was
Gray's desire to make this latter as much as possible like
the refined compositions of the Italian masters that he
loved, and Randall did his best to comply with this.   Gray
took great pains over the score, though in his private letters
he spoke with scorn of Randall's music ; but when he came
to the chorus, Gray remarked, " I have now done, make
as much noise as you please ! "   Dr. Burney, it afterwards
turned out, was very much disappointed because he was
not asked to set Gray's composition.   The *Installation Ode*
was performed before a brilliant assembly on July the 1st,
1769, Gray all the while sighing to be far away upon the
misty top of Skiddaw.   In the midst of all the turmoil
and circumstance of the installation he wrote in this way
to Norton Nicholls, who had consulted him about the
arrangement of his gardens :—

And so you have a garden of your own, and you plant and
transplant, and are dirty and amused ! Are you not ashamed
of yourself ? Why, I have no such thing, you monster, nor
ever shall be either dirty or amused as long as I live.   My

gardens are in the window, like those of a lodger up three
pairs of stairs in Petticoat Lane or Camomile Street, and they
go to bed regularly under the same roof that I do.   Dear,
how charming it must be to walk out in one's own *garding*,
and sit on a bench in the open air, with a fountain, and a
leaden statue, and a rolling stone, and an arbour : have a care
of sore throats, though, and the *agoe*.

It cannot be said that the *Installation Ode*, though it
contains some beautiful passages, is in Gray's healthiest
vein.   In it he returns, with excess, to that allegorical
style of his youth from which he had almost escaped, and
we are told a great deal too much about " painted Flattery "
and "creeping Gain," and visionary gentlefolks of that kind.
Where he gets free from all this, and especially in that
strophe when, after a silence of more than a century, we
hear once more the music of Milton's *Nativity Ode*, we
find him as charming as ever :—

> Ye brown, o'er-arching groves,
> That contemplation loves,
> Where willowy Camus lingers with delight !
> Oft at the blush of dawn
> I trod your level lawn,
> Oft woo'd the gleam of Cynthia silver-bright
> In cloisters dim, far from the haunts of Folly,
> With freedom by my side, and soft-eyed Melancholy.

The procession of Cambridge worthies, which Hallam has
praised so highly, is drawn with great dignity, and the
compliment conveyed in the sixth strophe, where the
venerable Margaret Beaufort bends from heaven to salute
her descendant, is very finely turned ; but we cannot help
feeling that the spirit of languor has not completely been
excluded from the poem, and that if Gray was not exhausted when he wrote it he was at least greatly fatigued.

The eulogy of the "star of Brunswick" at the close of the
Ode is perhaps the only absurd passage in the entire works
of Gray.   After this he wrote no verse that has been preserved; his faculty seems to have left him entirely, and if
we deplore his death within two years of the performance
of the *Installation Ode*, it is not without a suspicion that
the days of his poetic life were already numbered.

In 1769 Gray sold part of his estate, consisting of houses
on the west side of Hand Alley, in the City, for one
thousand guineas, and an annuity of eighty pounds for Mrs.
Oliffe, who had a share in the estate.   " I have also won
a twenty-pound prize in the lottery, and Lord knows what
arrears I have in the Treasury, and I am a rich fellow
enough, go to ; " so he writes on the 2nd of January of that
year to Norton Nicholls ; "and a fellow that hath had
losses, and one that hath two gowns, and everything handsome about him ; and in a few days I shall have curtains,
are you advised of that ? ay, and a mattress to lie upon."

One more work remained for Gray to do, and that a
considerable one.   He was yet to discover and to describe
the beauties of the Cumbrian Lakes.   In his youth he
was the man who first looked on the sublimities of Alpine
scenery with pleasure, and in old age he was to be the
pioneer of Wordsworth in opening the eyes of Englishmen
to the exquisite landscape of Cumberland.   The journal
of Gray's *Tour in the Lakes* has been preserved in full,
and was printed by Mason, who withheld his other itine-
raries.   He started from York, where he had been staying
with Mason, in July 1769, and spent the next two months
at Old Park.   On the 30th of September Gray found himself on the winding road looking westward, and with
Appleby and the long reaches of the Eden at his feet.   He
made no stay, but passed on to Penrith, for the night,

and in the afternoon walked up the Beacon Hill, and saw
"through an opening in the bosom of that cluster of
mountains the lake of Ulleswater, with the craggy tops of
a hundred nameless hills." Next day he ascended the
brawling bed of the Eamont, with the towers of Helvellyn
before him, until he reached Dunmallert. Gray's description of his first sight of Ulleswater, since sanctified to all
lovers of poetry by Wordsworth's *Daffodils*, is worth
quoting :—

Walked over a spongy meadow or two, and began to mount
this hill through a broad and straight green alley among the
trees, and with some toil gained the summit. From hence saw
the lake opening directly at my feet, majestic in its calmness,
clear and smooth as a blue mirror, with winding shores and
low points of land covered with green enclosures, white farm-
houses looking out among the trees, and cattle feeding. The
water is almost everywhere bordered with cultivated lands gently
sloping upwards till they reach the feet of the mountains, which
rise very rude and awful with their broken tops on either hand.
Directly in front, at better than three miles distance, Place
Fell, one of the bravest among them, pushes its bold broad
breast into the midst of the lake, and forces it to alter its course,
forming first a large bay to the left, and then bending to the
right.

It would seem that Wharton had been with his friend
during the first part of this excursion, but had been forced,
by a violent attack of asthma which came on at Brough,
to return home. It is to this circumstance alone that we
owe Gray's Journal, which was written piecemeal, and sent
by post to Wharton that he might share in what his friend
was doing. On the 1st of October Gray slept again at
Penrith, and set out early next morning for Keswick.
He passed at noon under the gleaming crags of Saddle-

back, the topmost point of which "appeared of a sad purple, from the shadow of the clouds as they sailed slowly by it." Passing by the mystery where Skiddaw shrouded "his double front among Atlantic clouds," Gray proceeded into Keswick, watching the sunlight reflected from the lake on every facet of its mountain-cup.

It seems that Gray walked about everywhere with that pretty toy, the Claude-Lorraine glass, in his hand, making the beautiful forms of the landscape compose in its lustrous chiaroscuro. Arranging his glass, in the afternoon of the 2nd of October, he got a bad fall backwards in a Keswick lane, but happily broke nothing but his knuckles. Next day, in company with the landlord of the Queen's Head, he explored the wonders of Borrowdale, the scene of Wordsworth's wild poem of *Yew Trees*. Just before entering the valley, he pauses to make a little vignette of the scene for Wharton's benefit :—

Our path here tends to the left, and the ground gently rising and covered with a glade of scattering trees and bushes on the very margin of the water, opens both ways the most delicious view, that my eyes ever beheld. Behind you are the magnificent heights of Walla Crag; opposite lie the thick hanging woods of Lord Egremont, and Newland Valley, with green and smiling fields embosomed in the dark cliffs; to the left the jaws of Borrowdale, with that turbulent chaos of mountain behind mountain rolled in confusion; beneath you, and stretching far away to the right, the shining purity of the lake, just ruffled with the breeze, enough to show it is alive, reflecting rocks, woods, fields, and inverted tops of mountains, with the white buildings of Keswick, Crossthwaite Church, and Skiddaw for a back-ground at a distance. Oh! Doctor, I never wished more for you.

All this is much superior in graphic power to what the

Paul Sandbys and Richard Wilsons could at that time
attain to in the art of painting. Their best landscapes, with
their sobriety and conscious artificiality, their fine tone
and studious repression of reality, are more allied to those
elegant and conventional descriptions of the picturesque
by which William Gilpin made himself so popular twenty
years later.   Even Smith of Derby, whose engravings of
Cumberland scenes had attracted notice, was tamely
topographical in his treatment of them.   Gray gives us
something more modern, yet no less exact, and reminds us
more of the early landscapes of Turner, with their
unaffected rendering of nature. Southey's early letters
from the Lakes, written nearly a generation later than
Gray's, though more developed in romantic expression,
are not one whit truer or more graphic.

Lodore seems to have been even in those days a sight
to which visitors were taken ; Gray gives a striking
account of it, but confesses that the crags of Gowder
were, to his mind, far more impressive than this slender
cascade.   The piles of shattered rock that hung above the
pass of Gowder gave him a sense of danger as well as of
sublimity, and reminded him of the Alps.   He glanced
at the balanced crags, and hurried on, whispering to himself " non ragionam di lor, ma guarda, e passa ! "   The
weather was most propitious ; if anything, too brilliantly
hot ; it had suggested itself to Gray that in such clear
weather and under such a radiant sky he ought to ascend
Skiddaw, but his laziness got the better of him, and he
judged himself better employed in sauntering along the
shore of Derwentwater :—

In the evening walked alone down to the Lake by the side of
Crow Park after sunset, and saw the solemn colouring of light
draw on, the last gleam of sunshine fading away on the hill-

tops, the deep serene of the waters, and the long shadows of the mountains thrown across them, till they nearly touched the hithermost shore.   At distance heard the murmur of many water-falls, not audible in the day-time.   Wished for the Moon, but she was *dark to me and silent, hid in her vacant interlunar cave*

Mr. Matthew Arnold has noticed that Gray has the accent of *Obermann* in such passages as these : it is the full tone of the romantic solitary without any of the hysterical over-gorgeousness which has ruined modern description of landscape.   The 4th of October was a day of rest ; the traveller contented himself with watching a procession of red clouds come marching up the eastern hills, and with gazing across the waterfall into the gorge of Borrowdale.   On the 5th he walked down the Derwent to Bassenthwaite Water, and skirmished a little around the flanks of Skiddaw ; on the 6th he drove along the eastern shore of Bassenthwaite towards Cockermouth, but did not reach that town, and returned to Keswick.   The next day, the weather having suddenly become chilly and autumnal, Gray made no excursions, but botanized along the borders of Derwentwater, with the perfume of the wild myrtle in his nostrils.   A little touch in writing to Wharton of the weather shows us the neat and fastidious side of Gray's character.   " The soil is so thin and light," he says of the neighbourhood of Keswick, " that no day has passed in which I could not walk out with ease, and you know I am no lover of dirt."   On the 8th he drove out of Keswick along the Ambleside road ; the wind was easterly and the sky grey, but just as they left the valley, the sun broke out, and bathed the lakes and mountain-sides with such a wonderful morning glory that Gray almost made up his mind to go back again.   He was particularly fascinated with the "clear obscure" of Thirlmere, shaded by the spurs of Helvellyn; and entering Westmoreland, descended into what Wordsworth was to make classic ground thirty years later, Grasmere,—

> Its crags, its woody steeps, its lakes,
> Its one green island, and its winding shores,
> The multitude of little rocky hills,
> Its church, and cottages of mountain stone,
> Clustered like stars.

This fragment of Wordsworth may be confronted by Gray's description of the same scene:—

Just beyond Helen Crag, opens one of the sweetest landscapes that art ever attempted to imitate. The bosom of the mountains, spreading here into a broad basin, discovers in the midst Grasmere Water; its margin is hollowed into small bays with bold eminences, some of them rocks, some of soft turf that half conceal and vary the figure of the little lake they command. From the shore a low promontory pushes itself far into the water, and on it stands a white village with the parish church rising in the midst of it; hanging enclosures, corn-fields, and meadows green as an emerald, with their trees, hedges, and cattle, fill up the whole space from the edge of the water. Just opposite to you is a large farmhouse at the bottom of a steep smooth lawn embosomed in old woods, which climb half-way up the mountainside, and discover above them a broken line of crags, that crown the scene. Not a single red tile, no flaring gentleman's house, or garden-walls, break in upon the repose of this little unsuspected paradise; but all is peace, rusticity, and happy poverty in its neatest and most becoming attire.

Passing from Grasmere, he drove through Rydal, not without a reference to the "large old-fashioned fabric, now a farm-house," which Wordsworth was to buy in 1813, and was to immortalize with his memory. I have not been

able to find any word in the writings of the younger poet
to show his consciousness of the fact that Gray's eye was
attracted to the situation of Rydal Mount exactly six
months before he himself saw the light at Cockermouth.
At Ambleside, then quite unprepared for the accommoda-
tion of strangers, Gray could find no decent bed, and so
went on to Kendal, for the first few miles skirting the
broad waters of Windermere, magnificent in the soft light
of afternoon. He spent two nights at Kendal, drove
round Morecambe Bay and slept at Lancaster on the
10th; reached Settle, under the "long black cloud of
Ingleborough," on the 12th; and we find him still wandering among the wild western moors of Yorkshire when
the journal abruptly closes on the 15th of October. On
the 18th he was once more at Aston with Mason, and
he returned to Cambridge on the 22nd, after a holiday of
rather more than three months.

CHAPTER IX.

GRAY became, in the last years of his life, an object of some curiosity at Cambridge. He was difficult of access, except to his personal friends. It was the general habit to dine in college at noon, so that the students might flock, without danger of indigestion, to the philosophical disputations at two o'clock. The fellows dined together in the Parlour, or the "Combination" as the common-room came to be called; and even when they dined in hall, they were accustomed to meet, in the course of the morning, over a seed-cake and a bottle of sherry-sack. But Gray kept aloof from these convivialities, at which indeed, as not being a fellow, he was not obliged to be present; and his dinner was served to him, by his man, in his own rooms. In the same way, when he was in town, at his lodgings in Jermyn Street, his meals were brought in to him from an eating-house round the corner. Almost the only time at which strangers could be sure of seeing him was when he went to the Rainbow coffee-house, at Cambridge, to order his books from the circulating library. The registers were kept by the woman at the bar, and no book was bought unless the requisition for it was signed by four subscribers. Towards the end of Gray's life, literary tuft-hunters used to contend for the

honour of supporting Gray's requests for books. There
was in particular a Mr. Pigott who desired to be thought
the friend of the poet, and who went so far as to erase the
next subscriber's name, and place his own underneath the
neat " T. Gray." It happened that Gray objected very
much to this particular gentleman, and he remarked one
day to his friend Mr. Sparrow, " That man's name
wherever I go, *piget*, he *Pigott's* me ! " It is said that
when Gray emerged from his chambers, graduates would
hastily leave their dinners to look at him, but we may
doubt, with Mr. Leslie Stephen, whether this is within
the bounds of probability ; Mathias, however, who would
certainly have left his dinner, was a whole year at Cambridge without being able to set eyes on Gray once. Lord
St. Helen's told Rogers that when he was at St. John's in
1770, he called on Gray with a letter of introduction, and
that Gray returned the call, which was thought so extraordinary, that a considerable number of college men
assembled in the quadrangle to see him pass, and all removed their caps when he went by. He brought three
young dons with him, and the procession walked in Indian
file ; his companions seem to have attended in silence,
and to have expressed dismay on their countenances when
Lord St. Helen's frankly asked the poet what he thought
of Garrick's *Jubilee Ode*,—which was just published. Gray
replied that he was easily pleased.

Unaffected to the extreme with his particular friends,
Gray seems to have adopted with strangers whom he
did not like, a supercilious air, and a tone of great
languor and hauteur. Cole, who did not appreciate him,
speaks, in an unpublished note, of his " disgusting
effeminacy," by which he means what we call affectation. Mason says that he used this manner as a

O

means of offence and defence towards persons whom he
disliked.   Here is a picture of him the year before
he died : " Mr. Gray's singular niceness in the choice
of his acquaintance makes him appear fastidious in
a great degree to all who are not acquainted with his
manner.   He is of a fastidious and recluse distance of
carriage, rather averse to all sociability, but of the graver
turn, nice and elegant in his person, dress, and behaviour,
even to a degree of finicality and effeminacy."   This
conception of him as an affected and effeminate little personage was widely current during his own lifetime.   Mr.
Penneck, the Superintendent of the Museum Reading-
Room, had a friend who travelled one day in the Windsor
stage with a small gentleman to whom, on passing Kensington Churchyard, he began to quote with great fervour
some stanzas of the *Elegy;* adding how extraordinary it was
that a poet of such genius and manly vigour of mind, should
be a delicate, timid, effeminate character, " in fact, sir," he
continued, " that Mr. Gray, who wrote those noble verses,
should be a puny insect shivering at a breeze."   The other
gentleman assented, and they passed to general topics, on
which he proved himself to be so well-informed, entertaining, and vivacious, that Penneck's friend was enchanted.   On leaving the coach, he fell into an enthusiastic
description of his fellow-traveller to the friend who met
him, and wound up by saying, " Ah ! here he is, returning
to the coach !   Who *can* he be ?"   " Oh ! that is Mr.
Gray, the poet ! "

Gray could be talkative enough in general society, if he
found the company sympathetic.   Walpole says that he
resembled Hume as a talker, but was much better company.   On one of his visits to Norton Nicholls at Blundeston, he found two old relatives of his host, people of the

most commonplace type, already installed, and at first he
seemed to consider it impossible to reconcile himself to
their presence. But noticing that Nicholls was grieved at
this, he immediately changed his manner, and made himself so agreeable to them both that the old people talked
of him with pleasure as long as they lived. He would
always interest himself in any reference to farming, or to
the condition of the crops, which bore upon his botanical
pursuits; one of his daily occupations, in his healthier
years, being the construction of a botanical calendar. One
of his finest sayings was:—" To be employed is to be
happy ;" and his great personal aim in life seems to have
been to be constantly employed, without fatigue, so as to
be able to stem the tide of constitutional low spirits. The
presence of his most intimate friends, such as Wharton
and Nicholls, had so magnetic an influence upon him, that
their memory of him was almost uniformly bright and
vivid.   Those whom he loved less, knew how dejected and
silent he could be for hours and hours.   Gibbon regretted
the pertinacity with which Gray plunged into merely
acquisitive and scholastic study ; the truth probably is,
that he had not the courage to indulge in reverie, nor the
physical health to be at rest.

The person, however, who has preserved the most exact
account of Gray's manner of life during the last months of
his career, is Bonstetten.   In November 1769 Norton
Nicholls, being at Bath, met in the Pump-Room there,
among the mob of fashionable people, a handsome young
Swiss gentleman of four-and-twenty, named Charles Victor
de Bonstetten. He was the only son of the treasurer of
Berne, and belonged to one of the six leading families of
the country.   He lived at Nyon, had been educated at
Lausanne, and was now in England, desiring to study our

language and literature, but having hitherto fallen more among fashionable people than people of taste. He was very enthusiastic, romantic, and good-looking, very sweet and winning in manner, full of wit and spirit, and, when he chose to exert himself, quite irresistible. He had brought an introduction to Pitt, but, after receiving some courtesies, had slipped away into the country, and Nicholls found him turning the heads of all the young ladies at Bath. Bonstetten attached himself very warmly to Nicholls, and was persuaded by the latter to go to Cambridge to attend lectures. That Nicholls thoroughly admired him, is certain from the very earnest letter of introduction which he sent with him to Gray on the 27th of November, 1769.

The ebullient young Swiss conquered the shy and solitary poet at sight. "My gaiety, my love for English poetry, appeared to have subdued him,"—the word Bonstetten uses is "subjugué,"—"and the difference in age between us seemed to disappear at once." Gray found him a lodging close to Pembroke Hall, at a coffee-house, and at once set himself to plan out for Bonstetten a course of studies. On the 6th of January, 1770, Bonstetten wrote to Norton Nicholls :—"I am in a hurry from morning till night. At eight o'clock I am roused by a young square-cap, with whom I follow Satan through chaos and night. . . We finish our travels in a copious breakfast of muffins and tea. Then appear Shakespeare and old Linnæus, struggling together as two ghosts would do for a damned soul. Sometimes the one gets the better, sometimes the other. Mr. Gray, whose acquaintance is my greatest debt to you, is so good as to show me Macbeth, and all witches, beldames, ghosts and spirits, whose language I never could have understood without his interpretation. I am now endeavouring to dress all these people in a French dress, which is a very hard labour." In enclosing this letter to Nicholls, Gray adds as a post-script :—

I never saw such a boy; our breed is not made on this model. He is busy from morning to night, has no other amusement than that of changing one study for another, likes nobody that he sees here, and yet wishes to stay longer, though he has passed a whole fortnight with us already. His letter has had no correction whatever, and is prettier by half than English.

For more than ten weeks after the date of this letter, Bonstetten remained in his lodgings at Cambridge, in daily and unbroken intercourse with Gray. The reminiscences of the young Swiss gentleman are extremely interesting, though doubtless they require to be accepted with a certain reservation. There is however the stamp of truth about his statement that the poetical genius of Gray was by this time so completely extinguished that the very mention of his poems was distasteful to him. He would not permit Bonstetten to talk to him about them, and when the young man quoted some of his lines, Gray preserved an obstinate silence like a sullen child. Sometimes Bonstetten said, " Will you not answer me ? " But no word would proceed from the shut lips. Yet this was during the time when, on all subjects but himself, Gray was conversing with Bonstetten on terms of the most affectionate intimacy. For three months the young Swiss, despising all other society to be found at Cambridge, spent every evening with Gray, arriving at five o'clock, and lingering till midnight. They read together Shakespeare, Milton, Dryden and the other great English classics, until their study would slip into sympathetic conversation, in

which the last word was never spoken.   Bonstetten poured
out his confidences to the old poet, — all his life, all his
hopes, all the aspirations and enthusiasms of his youth,
and Gray received it all with profound interest and
sympathy, but never with the least reciprocity.   To the
last his own life's history was a closed book to Bonstetten.
Never once did he speak of himself.   Between the present
and past there seemed to be a great gulf fixed, and when
the warm-hearted young man approached the subject, he
was always baffled.   He remarks that there was a complete
discord between Gray's humorous intellect and ardent
imagination on the one side and what he calls a "misère
de cœur" on the other.   Bonstetten thought that this was
owing to a suppressed sensibility, to the fact that Gray
never—

anywhere in the sun or rain
Had loved or been beloved again,

and that he felt his heart to be frozen at last under what
Bonstetten calls the Arctic Pole of Cambridge.

This final friendship of his life troubled the poet strangely.
He could not get over the wonder of Bonstetten's ardour
and vitality : "our breed is not made on this model."
His letters to Norton Nicholls are like the letters of an
anxious parent.   "He gives me," he says on the 20th of
March, 1770, "too much pleasure, and at least an equal
share of inquietude.   You do not understand him as well
as I do, but I leave my meaning imperfect, till we meet.
I have never met with so extraordinary a person.   God
bless him !   I am unable to talk to you about anything
else, I think."   Late in the month of March, Bonstetten
tore himself away from Cambridge ; his father had long
been insisting that he must return to Nyon.   Gray went
up to London with him, showed him some of the sights,

among others Dr. Samuel Johnson, who came puffing
down the Strand, unconscious of the two strangers who
paused on their way to observe him. "Look, look, Bonstetten!" said Gray, "the great Bear! There goes Ursa
Major!" On the 23rd of March Gray lent him 20*l.* and
packed his friend into the Dover machine at four o'clock
in the morning, returning very sadly to Cambridge, whence
he wrote to Nicholls:—"Here am I again to pass my
solitary evenings, which hung much lighter on my hands
before I knew him. This is your fault! Pray let the next
you send me be halt and blind, dull, unapprehensive and
wrong-headed. For this—as Lady Constance says—was
ever such a gracious creature born! and yet—but no
matter! . . . . . This place never appeared so horrible to
me as it does now. Could you not come for a week or
a fortnight? It would be sunshine to me in a dark
night."

Bonstetten had departed with every vow and circumstance of friendship, and had obliged Gray to promise that
he would visit him the next summer in Switzerland. He
wrote to Gray from Abbeville, and then there fell upon his
correspondence one of those silences so easy to the volatile
and youthful. Gray in the meanwhile was possessed by a
weak restlessness of mind that made him almost ill, and
early in April, since Nicholls could not come to Cambridge, he himself hastened to Blundeston, spending a few
days with Palgrave (" Old Pa ") on the way. He made
one excuse after another for avoiding Cambridge, to which
he did not return, except for a week or two, until the end
of the year. He agreed with Norton Nicholls that they
should go together to Switzerland in the summer of 1771,
but entreated him not to vex him by referring to this in
any way till the time came for starting. By and by letters

came from Bonstetten, with "bad excuses for not writing oftener," and in May Gray was happier, travelling to Aston to be with Mason, driving along the roads with trees blooming and nightingales singing all around him.

His only literary exercise during this year 1770 seems to have been filling an interleaved copy of the works of Linnæus with notes. For the last eight or nine years natural history had been his favourite study ; he said that it was a singular felicity to him to be engaged in this pursuit, and it often took him out into the fields when nothing else would. He interleaved a copy of Hudson's *Flora Anglica*, and filled it with notes : and was on a level with all that had been done up to his time in zoology and botany. Some of his notes and observations were afterwards made use of by Pennant, with warm acknowledgment. He returned from Aston towards the end of June, and prepared at once to start with Norton Nicholls for a summer tour. He directed Nicholls to meet him at the sign of the Wheat Sheaf, five miles beyond Huntingdon, about the 3rd of July. Unfortunately there exists no journal to commemorate this, the last of Gray's tours, which seems to have occupied more than two months. The friends drove across the midland counties into Worcestershire, descended the Severn to Gloucester, and then made their way to Malvern Wells, where they stayed a week, because Nicholls found some of his acquaintance there. Gray must have been particularly well, for he ascended the Herefordshire Beacon, and enjoyed the unrivalled view from its summit. He was much vexed, however, with the fashionable society at the long table of the inn, and maintained silence at dinner. When Nicholls gently rallied him on this, he said that long retirement in the university had destroyed

the versatility of his mind. At Malvern he received a
copy of Goldsmith's *Deserted Village*, which had just been
published ; he asked Norton Nicholls to read it aloud to
him, listened to it with fixed attention, and exclaimed
before they had proceeded far, "This man is a poet."
From Malvern they went on to Ross in Herefordshire,
and descended the Wye to Chepstow, a distance of forty
miles, in a boat, "surrounded," says Gray, "with ever new
delights." From this point they went on to Abergavenny
and South Wales, returning by Oxford, where they spent
two agreeable days. During this tour Gray turned aside
to visit Leasowes, where Shenstone had lived and died
in 1763. Gray had never admired Shenstone's artificial
grace, and had been vexed by some allusions in his
posthumously published letters, and it was probably more
to see the famous " Arcadian greens rural " than to do
homage to a poetic memory that he loitered at Halesowen.
He returned in a very fair state of health, as was customary
after his summer holidays ; but the good effects unfortunately passed away unusually soon. He had a feverish
attack in September, but cured it with sage-tea, his
favourite nostrum. Nicholls came up to town to see him,
and travelled with him as far as Cambridge; but Gray's now
invincible dislike to this place seems to have made him
really ill, and for the next two months he only went outside the walls of the college once. His aunt, Mrs. Oliffe,
now ninety years of age, had come up to Cambridge, and
appears to have lodged close to Gray inside Pembroke
College, where he was now allowed to do whatever he
chose. She was helplessly bedridden, but as intractable
a daughter of the Dragon of Wantley as ever. The other
Pembroke nonogenarian, Dr. Roger Long, died on the 16th
of December 1770, and Gray's friend James Brown suc-

ceeded him in the Mastership without any conten-
tion.

Early in 1771, Mrs. Oliffe died, leaving her entire fortune, such as it was, to Gray, and none of it to her nieces
the Antrobuses, who had nursed her in her illness.   These
women had been brought to Cambridge by Gray, and had
been so comfortably settled by him in situations, that in
one of his letters he playfully dreads that all his friends
will shudder at the name of Antrobus.   All through this
spring Gray seems to have been gradually sinking in
strength and spirits, though none of his friends appear to
have been alarmed about it.   To Norton Nicholls'
entreaties that he would go to visit Bonstetten with him,
as to the young Swiss gentleman's own invitations, he
answered with a sad intimation that his health was not
equal to so much exertion.

Nicholls came up to town to say farewell to him
in the middle of June, having at last been persuaded
that it was useless to wait for Gray.   The poet was
in his old rooms in Jermyn Street and there they parted
for the last time.   Before Nicholls took leave of him,
Gray said, very earnestly, "I have one thing to beg
of you, which you must not refuse."   Nicholls replied,
"You know you have only to command ; what is it ?"
"Do not go to visit Voltaire ; no one knows the mischief
that man will do."   Nicholls said, " Certainly I will not ;
but what could a visit from me signify ?"   " Every tribute
to such a man signifies."   A little before this Gray had
rejected polite overtures from Voltaire, who was a great
admirer of the *Elegy ;* but it was not that he was dead to
the charms of the great Frenchman.   He paid a full tribute
of admiration to his genius, delighted in his wit, enjoyed
his histories, and regarded his tragedies as next in rank

to those of Shakespeare ; but he hated him, as he hated
Hume, because, as he said, he thought him an enemy to
religion. He tried to persuade himself that Beattie had
mastered Voltaire in argumen⊥ Gray had a similar dislike to Shaftesbury, and was, t ghout his career, though
in a very unassuming way, , acere believer in Chris-
tianity. We find him exhorting Dr. Wharton not to omit
the use of family prayer, and this although he had a horror
of anything like " methodism " or religious display.

Gray's last letter to Bonstetten may be given as an
example of his correspondence with that gentleman, as
long after preserved and published by Miss Plumptre :—

I am returned, my dear Bonstetten, from the little journey I
made into Suffolk, without answering the end proposed. The
thought that you might have been with me there, has embittered
all my hours. Your letter has made me happy, as happy as so
gloomy, so solitary a being as I am, is capable of being made.
I know, and have too often felt, the disadvantages I lay myself
under ; how much I hurt the little interest I have in you by this
air of sadness so contrary to your nature and present enjoy-
ments : but sure you will forgive, though you cannot sympathize
with me. It is impossible with me to dissemble with you ;
such as I am I expose my heart to your view, nor wish to conceal a single thought from your penetrating eyes. All that you
say to me, especially on the subject of Switzerland, is infinitely
acceptable. It feels too pleasing ever to be fulfilled, and as
often as I read over your truly kind letter, written long since
from London, I stop at these words : " La mort qui peut glacer
nos bras avant qu'ils soient entrelacés."

He made a struggle to release himself from this atra-
bilious mood. He reflected on the business which he had
so long neglected, and determined to try again to find
energy to lecture. He drew up three schemes for regu-

lating the studies of private pupils, and laid them before
the Duke of Grafton.   But these plans, as was usual with
Gray, never came to execution, and when he was at Aston
in 1770, he told Mason that he had come to the conclusion
that it was his duty to resign the professorship, since it was
out of his power to do any real service in it.   Mason
strongly dissuaded him from such a step, and encouraged
him to think that even yet he would be able to make a
beginning of his lectures.   The Exordium of his proposed
inauguration speech was all that was found at his death to
account for so many efforts and intentions.

In the latter part of May 1771 Gray went up to London,
to his lodgings in Jermyn Street, where, as has been already
mentioned, he received the farewell visit from Nicholls.
He was profoundly wretched; writing to Wharton he
said, "Till this year I hardly knew what mechanical low
spirits were : but now I even tremble at an East wind."
His cough was incurable, the neuralgic pains in his head
were chronic.   William Robinson, in describing his last
interview with him, said that Gray talked of his own
career as a poet, lamented that he had done so little, and
began at last, in a repining tone, to complain that he had
lost his health just when he had become easy in his circumstances ; but on that he checked himself, saying that
it was wrong to rail against Providence.   As he grew
worse and worse, he placed himself under a physician,
Dr. Gisborne, who ordered him to leave Bloomsbury,
and try a clearer air at Kensington.   Probably the last
call he ever paid was on Walpole ; for hearing that his
old friend was about to set out for Paris, Gray visited
him.   "He complained of being ill," says Walpole, "and
talked of the gout in his stomach, but I expected his death
no more than my own."   During the month of June he

received the MS. of Gilpin's *Tour down the Wye*, and enriched this work, which was not published until 1782, with his notes, being reminiscences of his journey of the preceding year.

On the 22nd of July, finding himself alone in London, and overwhelmed with dejection and the shadow of death, he came back to Cambridge. It was his intention to rest there a day or two, and then to proceed to Old Park, where the Whartons were ready to receive him. He put himself under the treatment of his physician, Dr. Robert Glynn, who had been the author of a successful Seatonian poem, and who dabbled in literature. This Dr. Glynn was conspicuous for his gold-headed cane, scarlet coat, three-cornered hat, and resounding pattens for thirty years after Gray's death, and retains a niche in local history as the last functionary of the University who was buried by torchlight. Dr. Glynn was not at all anxious about Gray's condition, but on Wednesday the 24th, the poet was so languid, that his friend James Brown wrote for him to Dr. Wharton, to warn him that though Gray did not give over the hopes of taking his journey to Old Park, he was very low and feverish, and could hardly start immediately. That very night, while at dinner in the College Hall at Pembroke, Gray felt a sudden nausea, which obliged him to go hurriedly to his own room. He lay down, but he became so violently and constantly sick, that he sent his servant to fetch in Dr. Glynn, who was puzzled at the symptoms, but believed that there was no cause for alarm. Gray grew worse, however, for the gout had reached the stomach; Dr. Glynn became alarmed, and sent for Russell Plumptre, the Regius Professor of Physic. The old doctor was in bed, and refused to get up, for which he was afterwards severely blamed. No skill, however, could have saved Gray. He got through the 25th pretty well, and slept tolerably that night, but after taking some asses'-milk on the morning of the 26th, the spasms in the stomach returned again. Dr. Brown scarcely left him after the first attack, and wrote to all his principal friends from the side of his bed. On this day, Thursday, the Master could still hope " that we shall see him well again in a short time." On Sunday, the 29th, Gray was taken with a strong convulsive fit, and these recurred until he died. He retained his senses almost to the last. Stone-hewer and Dr. Gisborne arrived from London on the 30th and took leave of their dying friend. His language became less and less coherent, and he was not clearly able to explain to Brown, without a great effort, where his will would be found. He seemed perfectly sensible of his condition, but expressed no concern at the thought of leaving the world. Towards the end he did not suffer at all, but lay in a sort of torpor, out of which he woke to call for his niece, Miss Mary Antrobus. She took his hand, and he said to her, in a clear voice, " Molly, I shall die !" He lay quietly after this, without attempting to speak, and ceased to breathe about eleven o'clock, an hour before midnight on the 30th of July, 1771, aged fifty-four years, seven months, and four days.

James Brown found, in the spot which Gray had indicated, his will. It was dated July 2, 1770, and must therefore have been drawn up just before he started on his tour through the Western Counties. Mason and Brown were named his executors. He left his property divided among a great number of relations and friends, reserving the largest portions for his niece Miss Mary Antrobus, and her sister, Mrs. Dorothy Comyns, both of whom were residents at Cambridge, and who had probably looked to his comfort of late years as he had considered their prospects in earlier life. The faithful Stephen Hempstead was not forgotten, while Mason and Brown were left residuary legatees. On Brown fell the whole burden of attending to the funeral, for Mason could not be found; he had taken a holiday, and knew nothing of the whole matter until his letters reached him, in a cluster, at Bridlington Quay, about the 7th of August.

By this time Gray was buried; Brown took the body, in a coffin of seasoned oak, to London and thence to Stoke, where, on the 6th of August, it was deposited in the vault which contained that of Gray's mother. The mourners were Miss Antrobus, her sister's husband, Mr. Comyns, a shopkeeper at Cambridge, "a young gentleman of Christ's College, with whom Mr. Gray was very intimate," and Brown himself; these persons followed the hearse in a mourning coach. The sum of ten pounds was, at the poet's express wish, distributed among certain "honest and industrious poor persons in the parish" of Stoke Pogis. As soon as Mason heard the news, he crossed the Humber, and reached Cambridge the next day; Brown was a very cautious and punctilious man, and no sooner had he returned to Cambridge than he insisted that Mason should go up to town with him and prove the will. Mason, who throughout showed a characteristic callousness, grumbled but agreed, and on the 12th of August the will was proved in London.

The executors returned immediately to Cambridge, delivered up the plate, jewellery, linen, and furniture to the Antrobuses, and then Mason packed up the books and papers to be removed to his rooms at York. Once settled there, on the 18th, he began to enjoy the luxury of a literary bereavement. "Come," he says to Dr. Wharton, " come, I beseech you, and condole with me on our mutual, our irreparable loss. The great charge which his dear friendship has laid upon me, I feel myself unable to execute, without the advice and assistance of his best friends ; you are among the first of these." It will hardly be believed that the " great charge " so pompously referred to here is contained in these exceedingly simple words of Gray :—" I give to the Reverend William Mason, precentor of York, all my books, manuscripts, coins, music printed or written, and papers of all kinds, to preserve or destroy at his own discretion." There is no shadow of doubt that the ambitious and worldly Mason saw here an opportunity of achieving a great literary success, and that he lost no time in posing as Gray's representative and confidant. A few people resisted his pretensions, such as Robinson and Nicholls, but they were not writers, and Mason revenged himself by ignoring them. Nor did he take the slightest notice of Bonstetten.

James Brown, *le petit bon homme* with the warm heart, was kinder and less ambitious. He wrote thoughtful letters to every one, and particularly to the three friends in exile, to Horace Walpole, Nicholls, and Bonstetten. Walpole was struck cold in the midst of his frivolities, as if he had suffered in his own person a touch of paralysis; in his letters he seems to whimper and shiver, as much with apprehension as with sorrow. Norton Nicholls gave a cry of grief, and very characteristically wrote instantly to his mother lest she, knowing his love for Gray, should fear that the shock would make him ill. From this exquisite letter we must cite some lines :—

I only write now lest you should be apprehensive on my

account since the death of my dear friend.　Yesterday's post
brought me the fatal news, in a letter from Mr. Brown, that
Mr. Gray (all that was most dear to me in this world except
yourself) died in the night about eleven o'clock, between the
30th and 31st of July. . . .　You need not be alarmed for me,
I am well, and not subject to emotions violent enough to en-
danger my health, and besides with good kind people who pity
me and can feel themselves.　Afflicted you may be sure I am!
You who know I considered Mr. Gray as a second parent, that
I thought only of him, built all my happiness on him, talked of
him for ever, wished him with me whenever I partook of any
pleasure, and flew to him for refuge whenever I felt any un-
easiness; to whom now shall I talk of all I have seen here?
Who will teach me to read, to think, to feel?　I protest to you,
that whatever I did or thought had a reference to him,—" Mr.
Gray will be pleased with this when I tell him.　I must ask
Mr. Gray what he thinks of such a person or thing.　He would
like such a person or dislike such another."　If I met with any
chagrins, I comforted myself that I had a treasure at home; if
all the world had despised and hated me, I should have thought
myself perfectly recompensed in his friendship.　Now remains
only one loss more; if I lose *you*, I am left alone in the world.
At present I feel I have lost half of myself.　Let me hear that
you are well.

Thirty-four years afterwards the hand which penned
these unaffected lines wrote down those reminiscences, alas!
too brief, which constitute the most valuable impressions
of Gray that we possess.　It is impossible not to regret
that this sincere and tender friend did not undertake that
labour of biography which fell into more skilled, but
coarser hands than his.　Yet it is no little matter to
possess this first outflow of grief and affection.　It
assures us that, with all his melancholy and self-
torture, the great spirit of Gray was not without its
lively consolations, and that he gained of Heaven

P

the boon for which he had prayed, a friend of friends.
Nicholls, Bonstetten, Robinson, Wharton, Stonehewer,
and Brown were undistinguished names of unheroic
men who are interesting to posterity only because, with
that unselfish care which only a great character and sweetness of soul have power to rouse, they loved, honoured,
cherished this silent and melancholy anchorite. Dearer
friends, better and more devoted companions through a
slow and unexhilarating career, no man famous in literature
has possessed, and we feel that not to recognize this magnetic power of attracting good souls around him would be
to lose sight of Gray's peculiar and signal charm. It is
true that, like the moon, he was "dark to them, and
silent;" that he received, and lacked the power to give;
they do not seem to have required from him the impossible,
they accepted his sympathy, and rejoiced in his inexpres-
sive affection; and when he was taken from them, they
regarded his memory as fanatics regard the sayings and
doings of the founder of their faith. Gray "never spoke
out," Brown said; he lived, more even than the rest of us,
in an involuntary isolation, a pathetic type of the solitude
of the soul.

> Yes! in the sea of life enisled,
> With echoing straits between us thrown,
> Dotting the shoreless watery wild,
> We mortal myriads live *alone*.
> The islands feel the enclasping flow,
> And then their endless bounds they know.

CHAPTER X.

THE earliest tribute to the mind and character of Gray was published in 1772 in the March number of a rather dingy periodical, issued under Dr. Johnson's protection, and entitled the *London Magazine.* This was written in the form of a letter to Boswell by a man who had little sympathy with Gray as a poet or as a wit, but was well fitted to comprehend him as a scholar, the Reverend William J. Temple, vicar of St. Gluvias. This gentleman, who had been a fellow of Trinity Hall during Gray's residence in Cambridge, and who is frequently mentioned in the poet's later letters, was almost the only existing link between the circles ruled respectively by Gray and Samuel Johnson, Cole being perhaps the one other person known to both these mutually repellent individuals. Temple's contribution to the *London Magazine* is styled " A Sketch of the Character of the Celebrated Poet Mr. Gray," and is ushered in by the editor with some perfunctory compliments to the poems. But Temple's own remarks are very valuable, and may be reprinted here, especially as the careful Mitford and every succeeding writer seem to have been content to quote them from Johnson's inaccurate transcript :—

Perhaps Mr. Gray was the most learned man in Europe : he was equally acquainted with the elegant and profound parts of Science, and not superficially, but thoroughly. He knew every

branch of history, both natural and civil; had read all the
original historians of England, France, and Italy; and was a
great antiquarian.   Criticism, metaphysics, morals, politics,
made a principal part of his plan of study.   Voyages and travels
of all sorts were his favourite amusement: and he had a fine
taste in painting, prints, architecture, and gardening.   With such
a fund of knowledge, his conversation must have been equally
instructing and entertaining.   But he was also a good man, a
well-bred man, a man of virtue and humanity.   There is no character without some speck, some imperfection; and I think the
greatest defect in his, was an affectation in delicacy or rather
effeminacy, and a visible fastidiousness or contempt and disdain
of his inferiors in science.   He also had in some degree that
weakness which disgusted Voltaire so much in Mr. Congreve.
Though he seemed to value others chiefly according to the progress they had made in knowledge, yet he could not bear to be
considered himself merely as a man of letters: and though without birth, or fortune, or station, his desire was to be looked
upon as a private gentleman, who read for his amusement."

Against the charge of priggishness which seems to be
contained in these last lines, we may place Norton
Nicholls' anecdote, that having in the early part of their
acquaintance remarked that some person was "a clever
man," he was cut short by Gray, who said, "Tell me if
he is good for anything."   Another saying of his, that
genius and the highest acquirements of science were as
nothing compared with "that exercise of right reason
which Plato called virtue," is equally distinct as evidence
that he did not place knowledge above conduct.   But the
earlier part of Temple's article, which regards Gray's learning and acquisitions of every sort, is of great value.
Another of the poet's contemporaries, Robert Potter, the
translator of Æschylus, and one of the foremost scholars of
the time, followed with a similar statement.   " Mr. Gray

was perhaps the most learned man of the age, but his
mind never contracted the rust of pedantry.   He had too
good an understanding to neglect that urbanity which
renders society pleasing : his conversation was instructing,
elegant, and agreeable.   Superior knowledge, an exquisite
taste in the fine arts, and, above all, purity of morals, and
an unaffected reverence for religion, made this excellent
person an ornament to society, and an honour to human
nature."

Mason lost no time in giving out that he was collecting
materials for a Life of Gray.   His first literary act was to
print for private circulation in 1772 the opening book of his
didactic poem *The English Garden*, which he had written
as early as 1767, but which Gray had never allowed him
to print, speaking freely of it as being nonsense.   But
Mason loved the children of his brain, and could not support the idea that one of them should be withheld from
the world.   With great naïveté, he attempted to argue
the matter with the shade of his great friend in a third
book which he added in 1772.

> Clos'd is that curious ear, by Death's cold hand,
> That mark'd each error of my careless strain
> With kind severity; to whom my Muse
> Still lov'd to whisper what she meant to sing
> In louder accent; to whose taste supreme
> She first and last appealed,

but still the departed friend may be invoked by the Muse,

> and still, by Fancy sooth'd,
> Fain would she hope her GRAY attends the call.

Mason then refers, in the flat, particular manner native to
eighteenth century elegy, to the urn and bust and sculp-
tured lyre which he had placed to the memory of Gray in

a rustic alcove in the garden at Aston, and then he ap-
proaches the awkward circumstance that Gray considered
The English Garden trash :—

> Oft, " smiling as in scorn," oft would he cry,
> " Why waste thy numbers on a trivial art
> That ill can mimic even the humblest charms
> Of all-majestic Nature ? " at the word
> His eye would glisten, and his accents glow
> With all the Poet's frenzy; " Sovereign Queen !
> Behold, and tremble, while thou viewest her State
> Thron'd on the heights of Skiddaw : trace her march
> Amid the purple crags of Borrowdale.
> .   .   .   . Will thy boldest song
> E'er brace the sinews of enervate art
> To such dread daring ?   Will it e'en direct
> Her hand to emulate those softer charms
> That deck the banks of Dove, or call to birth
> The bare romantic crags," &c.

It seems highly probable that, stripped of the charms of
blank verse, this is precisely what Gray was constantly
saying to Mason, who greatly preferred artificial cascades
and myrtle grots to all the mountains in Christendom.
On the fly-leaf of this private edition of *The English
Garden* in 1772 appeared the first general announcement
of the coming biography.

The work progressed very slowly.   From the family of
West, who had now been dead thirty years, Mason was
fortunate enough to secure a number of valuable letters,
but it was difficult to fill up the hiatus between the close
of this correspondence and the beginning of Mason's personal acquaintance with Gray.   Wharton and Horace
Walpole came very kindly to his aid, and he was able to
collect a considerable amount of material.   It is dis-
tressing to think of the mass of papers, letters, verses,

and other documents which Mason possessed, and of the comparatively small use which he made of them. He conceived the happy notion, which does not seem to have been thought of by any previous writer, of allowing Gray to tell his own story by means of his letters ; but he vitiated the evidence so put before the world by tampering grossly with the correspondence. He confessed to Norton Nicholls, who was angry at this, that " much liberty was taken in transposing parts of the letters," but he did not go on to mention that he allowed himself to interpolate and erase passages, to conceal proper names, to mutilate the original MSS., and to alter dates and opinions. He was very anxious that what he called his " fidelity " should not " be impeached " to the public and the critics, but declared that he had only acted for the honour of Gray himself. It is probable that in his foolish heart Mason really did consider that he was respecting Gray in thus brushing his clothes and washing his hands for him before allowing the world to see him. He thought that a ruffled wig or a disordered shoe-tie would destroy his hero's credit with the judicious, and accordingly he removed all that was silly and natural from the letters. This determination to improve Gray has marred, also, the slender thread of biography by which the letters are linked together, yet to a less degree than might be supposed, and the student finds himself constantly returning to Mason's meagre and slipshod narrative for some fact which has been less exactly stated by the far more careful and critical Mitford. Mason had too much literary ability, and had known Gray too intimately and too long, to make his book other than valuable. It is faulty and unfinished, but it is a sketch from the life. It appeared, in two quarto volumes, in

June 1775 and was received with great warmth by the
critics, the public, and all but the intimate friends of
Gray. Mason often reprinted this book, which continued to be a sort of classic until Mitford commenced his
investigations.

It has generally been acknowledged that Johnson's Life
of Gray is the worst section in his delightful series. It
formed the last chapter but one in the fourth volume of the
Lives of the Poets, and was written when its author was tired
of his task, and longing to be at rest again. It is barren
and meagre of fact to the last degree ; Cole, the antiquary,
gave into Johnson's charge a collection of anecdotes and
sayings of Gray which he had formed in connexion with
the poet's Cambridge friends, especially Tyson and Sparrow, but the lexicographer was disinclined to make any
use of them, and they were dispersed and lost. We have
already seen that these two great men, the leading men of
letters of their age in England, were radically wanting in
sympathy. Gray disliked Johnson personally, apparently
preserving the memory of some chance meeting in which the
Sage had been painfully self-asserting and oppressive ; he
was himself a lover of limpid and easy prose, and a master
of the lighter parts of writing, and therefore condemned the
style of Dr. Johnson hastily, as being wholly turgid and
vicious. Yet he respected his character, and has recorded
the fact that Johnson often went out in the streets of
London with his pockets full of silver, and had given it
all away before he returned home.

Johnson's portrait of Gray is somewhat more judicial than
this, but just as unsympathetic. Yet he made one remark,
after reading a few of Gray's letters, which seems to me to
surpass in acumen all the generalities of Mason, namely that
though Gray was fastidious and hard to please, he was a

man likely to love much where he loved at all. But for Gray's poems Johnson had little but bewilderment. If they had not received the warm sanction of critics like Warburton and Hurd, and the admiration of such friends of his own as Boswell and Garrick, it seems likely that Johnson would not have acknowledged in them any merit whatever. Where he approves of them, no praise could be fainter; where he objects, he is even more trenchant and contemptuous than usual. The *Elegy in a Country Churchyard*, and the *Ode on Adversity* are the only pieces in the whole repertory of Gray to which he allows the tempered eulogy that he is not willing to withhold from Mallet or Shenstone. We shall probably acquit the sturdy critic of any unfairness, even involuntary, when we perceive that for the poetry of Collins, who was his friend and the object of his benefactions, he has even less toleration than for the poetry of Gray.

When we examine Johnson's strictures more exactly still, we find that the inconsistency which usually accompanied the expression of his literary opinions does not forsake him here. Even when Johnson is on safe ground, as when he is weighing in a very careful balance the *Epitaphs* of Pope, he is never a sure critic; he brings his excellent common sense to bear on the subject in hand, but is always in too great haste to be closing not to omit some essential observation. But when discussing poetry so romantic in its nature as that of Gray, he deals blows even more at random than usual. The *Ode on Adversity* meets with his warmest approbation, and he suggests no objection to its allegorical machinery, to much of which no little exception might now be taken. But the *Eton Ode*, with strange want of caution, he declaims against in detail, blaming at one time what posterity

is now content to admire, and at the other what his own
practice in verse might have amply justified. " The
Prospect of Eton College suggests nothing to Gray, which
every beholder does not equally think and feel," that is to
say, which every susceptible and cultivated beholder does
not feel in a certain vein of reflection; but this, so far
from being a fault, is the touch of nature which makes the
poem universally interesting. " His supplication to Father
Thames, to tell him who drives the hoop or tosses the
ball, is useless and puerile. Father Thames has no better
means of knowing than himself." In this case, Johnson
was instantly reminded that Father Nile had been called
upon for information exactly analogous in the pages of
Rasselas. " His epithet *buxom health* is not elegant," but
to us it seems appropriate, which is better. Finally Johnson finds that " redolent of joy and youth " is an expression removed beyond apprehension, and is an imitation
of a phrase of Dryden's misunderstood; but here Gray
proves himself the better scholar. It may be conjectured
that he found this word *redolent,* of which he was particularly fond, among the old Scots poets of the sixteenth
century, whom he was the first to unearth. Dunbar and
Scot love to talk of the " redolent rose."

The phrases above quoted constitute Johnson's entire
criticism of the *Eton Ode,* and it is of a kind, which however
vigorously expressed, would not now-a-days be considered
competent before the least accredited of tribunals. The
examination of the two Pindaric odes is conducted on more
conscientious but not more sympathetic principles. To the
experiments in metre, to the verbal and quantitative felicities,
Johnson is absolutely deaf. He does not entirely deny merit
to the poems, but he contrives, most ingeniously, to hesitate contempt. " My process," he says, " has now brought
me to the wonderful Wonder of Wonders, the two Sister

Odes; by which, though either vulgar ignorance or
common sense at first universally rejected them, many
have been since persuaded to think themselves delighted.
I am one of those that are willing to be pleased, and therefore would gladly find the meaning of the first stanza
of the *Progress of Poetry.*" Johnson, it is obvious
enough, is on the side of "common sense." The difficulty which he was pleased to find in the opening
stanza of the ode is one which he would have been the
first to denounce as whimsical and paltry if brought forward by some other critic. Gray describes the formation
of poetry under the symbol of a widening river, calm and
broad in its pastoral moments, loud, riotous and resonant
when swollen by passion or anger. Johnson, to whom the
language of Greek poetry and the temper of Greek thought
were uncongenial, refused to grasp this direct imagery, and
said that if the poet was speaking of music, the expression
"rolling down the steep amain" was nonsense, and if of
water, nothing to the point. So good a scholar should
have known, and any biographer should have noticed that
Gray had pointed out, that, as usual in Pindar, whom he is
here closely paraphrasing, the subject and simile are united.
Johnson was careless enough to blame Gray for inventing
the compound adjective *velvet-green*, although Pope and
Young, poets after Johnson's own heart, had previously
used it. The rest of his criticism is equally faulty, and
from the same causes,—haste, and want of sympathy.

Johnson's attack did nothing at first to injure Gray's
position as a poet. Yet there can be no doubt that in
the process of time, the great popularity of the *Lives of
the Poets*, and the oblivion into which Mason's life has
fallen, have done something sensibly to injure Gray with
the unthinking. Even in point of history the life of
Gray is culpably full of errors, and might as well have

been written if Mason's laborious work had never been published. There is, however, one point on which Johnson did early justice to Gray, and that is in commending the picturesque grace of his descriptions of the country. Against the condemnation of Johnson, there were placed, almost instantly, the enthusiastic praises of Adam Smith, Gibbon, Hume, Mackintosh, and others of no less authority, who were unanimous in ranking his poetry only just below that of Shakespeare and Milton. This view continued until the splendours of the neo-romantic school, especially the reputations of Wordsworth and Byron, reduced the luminary and deprived it of its excess of light. The Lake School, particularly Coleridge, professed that Gray had been unfairly over-rated, and it was rather Byron and Shelley who sustained his fame, as in some directions they continued his tradition.

It would be to leave this little memoir imperfect if we did not follow the destinies of that group of intimate friends who survived the poet, and whose names are indissolubly connected with his. The one who died first was Lord Strathmore, who passed away, prematurely, in 1776. James Brown continued to hold the mastership of Pembroke, and to enjoy the reputation of a gentle and good-natured old man until 1784, when he followed his friend to the grave. Young men of letters, such as Sir Egerton Brydges, considered it a privilege to be asked to the Master's Lodge, and to take tea with the man in whose arms Gray breathed his last, although Brown had no great power of reminiscence, and had not much to tell such eager questioners. Of himself it was told that his ways were so extremely punctilious as to amuse Gray, himself a very regular man, and that once, when the friends were going to start together at a certain hour, and the time had just arrived, Brown rose and began to walk to and fro,

whereupon Gray exclaimed, " Look at Brown, he is going
to strike ! "   Dr. Thomas Wharton (who must never be
confounded with Thomas Warton, the poet-laureate) continued to live at his house at Old Park, Durham, where
Gray had so often spent delightful weeks.   He died in
1794 at a great age, and left his ample correspondence
with Gray to his second son, a man of some literary pretensions, of whom Sir Egerton Brydges has given an interesting account.   Mason and Walpole, whose careers are
too well known to be dwelt upon here, survived their celebrated friend by more than a quarter of a century.   Horace
Walpole died on March 2, and Mason on April 4, 1797.

At the close of the century several of Gray's early
friends still survived.   The Rev. William Robinson,
having reached the age of seventy-six, died in December
1803.   On his tomb in the church of Monk's Horton, in
Kent, it was stated that he was " especially intimate with
the poet Gray," with whom he probably became acquainted
through the accident that his mother, after his father's
death, made Dr. Conyers Middleton her second husband.
His sister was the Mrs. Elizabeth Montagu who wrote the
Essay on Shakespeare and who patronized Dr. Johnson.
The kind and faithful Stonehewer died at a very advanced age in 1809, bequeathing to Pembroke Hall those
commonplace-books of Gray's from which Mathias reaped
his bulky volumes, and yet left much for me to glean.
Norton Nicholls died rector of Lound and Bradwell in
Suffolk, on the 22nd of November, in the same year, 1809,
having fortunately placed on paper, four years before, his
exquisite reminiscences of Gray.   He also bears on his
memorial tablet, in Richmond Church, his claim to the
regard of posterity : " He was the friend of the illustrious
Gray."

The most remarkable, certainly the most original,

of Gray's friends, was also.the most long-lived.   Charles
Victor de Bonstetten had but just begun his busy and
eccentric career when he crossed the orbit of Gray.   He
lived not merely to converse with Byron but to survive
him, and to see a new age of literature inaugurated.   He
was a copious writer, and his works enjoyed a certain
vogue.   His well-known description of Gray occurs in a
book of studies published in 1831, the year before he
died, *Les Souvenirs du Chevalier de Bonstetten.*   In the
most chatty of his books, *L'Homme du Midi et l'homme
du Nord,* he says that he found in England that friendship
of the most intimate kind could subsist between persons
who were satisfied to remain absolutely silent in one
another's presence ; there may be a touch of the reserve
of Gray in this vague allusion.

In Bonstetten the romantic seed which Gray may
be supposed to have sown, burst into extravagant
blossom.   His conduct in private life seems, from
what can be gathered, to have been founded on a
perusal of *La Nouvelle Heloise,* and though he was
a pleasant little fat man, with rosy cheeks, his conduct was hardly up to the standard which Gray would
have approved of.   Bonstetten may perhaps be described
as a smaller Benjamin Constant ; like him, he was Swiss
by birth, first roused to intellectual interest in England,
and finally sentimentalized in Germany ; but he was not
quite capable of writing *Adolphe.*   Bonstetten followed
Gray in studying the Scandinavian tongues ; he acquainted
himself with Icelandic, and wrote copiously, though not very
wisely, on the Eddas.   He brought out a German edition
of his works at Copenhagen, where he spent some time,
and whither he pursued his eccentric friend Matthison.
Bonstetten died at Genoa in February, 1832, at the age of
eighty-seven.   The last survivor among people whom

Gray knew was probably the Earl of Burlington, "little brother George," who died in 1834. Perhaps the last person who was certainly in Gray's presence was Sir Samuel Egerton Brydges, who was present, at the age of three, at a wedding at which Gray assisted, and who died in 1837.

Gray was rather short in stature, of graceful build in early life, but too plump in later years. He walked in a wavering and gingerly manner, the result probably of weakness. Besides the portraits already described in the body of this memoir, there is a painting at Pembroke Hall by Benjamin Wilson, F.R.S., a versatile artist whose work was at one time considered equal to that of Hogarth. This portrait is in profile; it was evidently painted towards the close of the poet's life; the cheeks are puffed, and the lips have fallen inwards through lack of teeth. Gray is also stated to have sat to one of the Vanderguchts, but this portrait seems to have disappeared. In 1778 Mason commissioned the famous sculptor John Bacon, who was just then executing various works in Westminster Abbey, to carve the medallion now existing in Poet's Corner; as Bacon had never seen Gray, Mason lent him a profile drawing by himself, the original of which, a hideous little work, is now preserved at Pembroke. A bust of Gray, by Behnes, founded on the full-face portrait by Eckhardt, stands with those of other famous scholars, in Upper School at Eton.

In 1776, according to a College Order which Mr. J. W. Clark has kindly copied for me, "James Brown, Master, and William Mason, Fellow, each gave fifty pounds to establish a building fund in memory of Thomas Gray the Poet, who had long resided in the College." The fund so started gradually accumulated until it amounted to a very large sum. Certain alterations were made, but nothing serious was attempted until, about thirty years ago, Mr. Cory, a fellow of Emmanuel College, took down the Christopher Wren doorway to the hall, and attempted to harmonise the whole structure to Gothic. Still the Gray Building Fund was accumulating, and the college was becoming less and less able to accommodate its inmates. It was determined at last to carry out the scheme proposed nearly a century before by Brown and Mason. In March 1870, the work was put into the hands of Mr. Alfred Waterhouse. He was at work on the college until 1879, and in his hands if it is no longer picturesque it is thoroughly comfortable and habitable.

In all this vast expenditure of money, not one penny was spent, until quite lately, in commemoration of the man in whose name it was collected. At Peterhouse, when the College Hall was restored in 1870, a stained glass window, drawn by Mr. F. Madox Brown and executed by Mr. William Morris, was presented by Mr. A. H. Hunt. At Pembroke a still more fitting memorial was erected on the 26th of May 1885, when a marble bust by Mr. Hamo Thornycroft, A.R.A., was unveiled by Lord Houghton in the College Hall in the presence of a very distinguished audience. Mr. Lowell and Sir Frederick Leighton, among others, gave eloquent testimony on that occasion to the lasting esteem in which the memory of Gray is held on both sides of the Atlantic.

THE END.

APPENDIX

It was not known until the Dillon MSS. passed through my hands in 1884 that in August 1764, about a month after the surgical operation which is described on p. 165, Gray went to Netherby, on the Scotch border, to visit the Rev. Mr. Graham, the horticulturist, and from his house set out on a tour through Scotland. His route took him by Annan and Dumfries to the Falls of the Clyde and Lanark. At Glasgow he visited Foulis, the publisher, from whom he afterwards received many courtesies. He admired Foulis' academy of painting and sculpture, and lamented that the Cathedral of Glasgow had fallen so much out of repair. He passed on to Loch Lomond, sailed on the loch, and returned to Glasgow by Dumbarton. At Stirling he enjoyed the view from the Castle, and went on by Falkirk and the coast to Edinburgh. He took excursions to Hawthornden and Roslin, and thence to Melrose. He was next at Kelso, Tweedmouth, and Norham Castle. He made an excursion at low tide to Holy Island, and the journal closes at Bamborough Castle, from which place he went, no doubt, to his customary haunt, Dr. Wharton's house at Old Park, in the county of Durham. This was Gray's first visit to Scotland.